DATA MINING AND BUSINESS INTELLIGENCE

QUESTIONS, ANSWERS, & EVERYTHING IN BETWEEN

BY MOHIT THAKKAR

About the Book:

It often happens that when we try to study a subject for some examination or a job interview, we just don't find the right content.

The problem with the reference books is that they are too descriptive for last moment studies. Whereas the problem with local publications is that they are inaccurate as compared to the reference books.

This particular book encapsulates the subject notes on **Data Mining & Business Intelligence** with the combined benefits of reference books & local publications. It has the accuracy of a reference book as well as the abstraction of a local publication.

The author studied the subject from various sources such as web lectures, reference books, online tutorials & so on. After having a thorough understanding of the subject, the author compiled this book for an easy understanding of the subject.

This book presents the content in the form of question & answers, with utmost simplicity of language, and in an abstract manner so that it can be used for last moment studies. This book can be used by:

➢ Students to prepare for their examinations

➢ Professionals to prepare for job interviews.

➢ Individuals willing to have a basic understanding of the domain: Data Mining & Business Intelligence.

Happy Reading!

References:

1. Data Mining Concepts and Techniques - J. Han, M. Kamber, Morgan Kaufmann – (3rd Edition) – Elsevier Inc.

2. Data mining: Concepts, models, methods and algorithms – M. Kantardzic - John Wiley & Sons Inc.

Disclaimer:

Contents:

Contents:

List of Figures:

Q1. Draw and explain the data warehouse architecture.

A **business analyst** get the information from the **data warehouses** to **measure the performance** and make critical adjustments to a **business**. Having a **data warehouse** offers the following **advantages**:

- o Since a data warehouse can **gather information quickly and efficiently**, it can **enhance business productivity**.

- o A data warehouse provides us a **consistent view of customers and items**; hence, it helps us **manage customer relationship**.

- o A data warehouse also helps in bringing down the costs by **tracking trends, patterns** over a long period in a consistent and reliable manner.

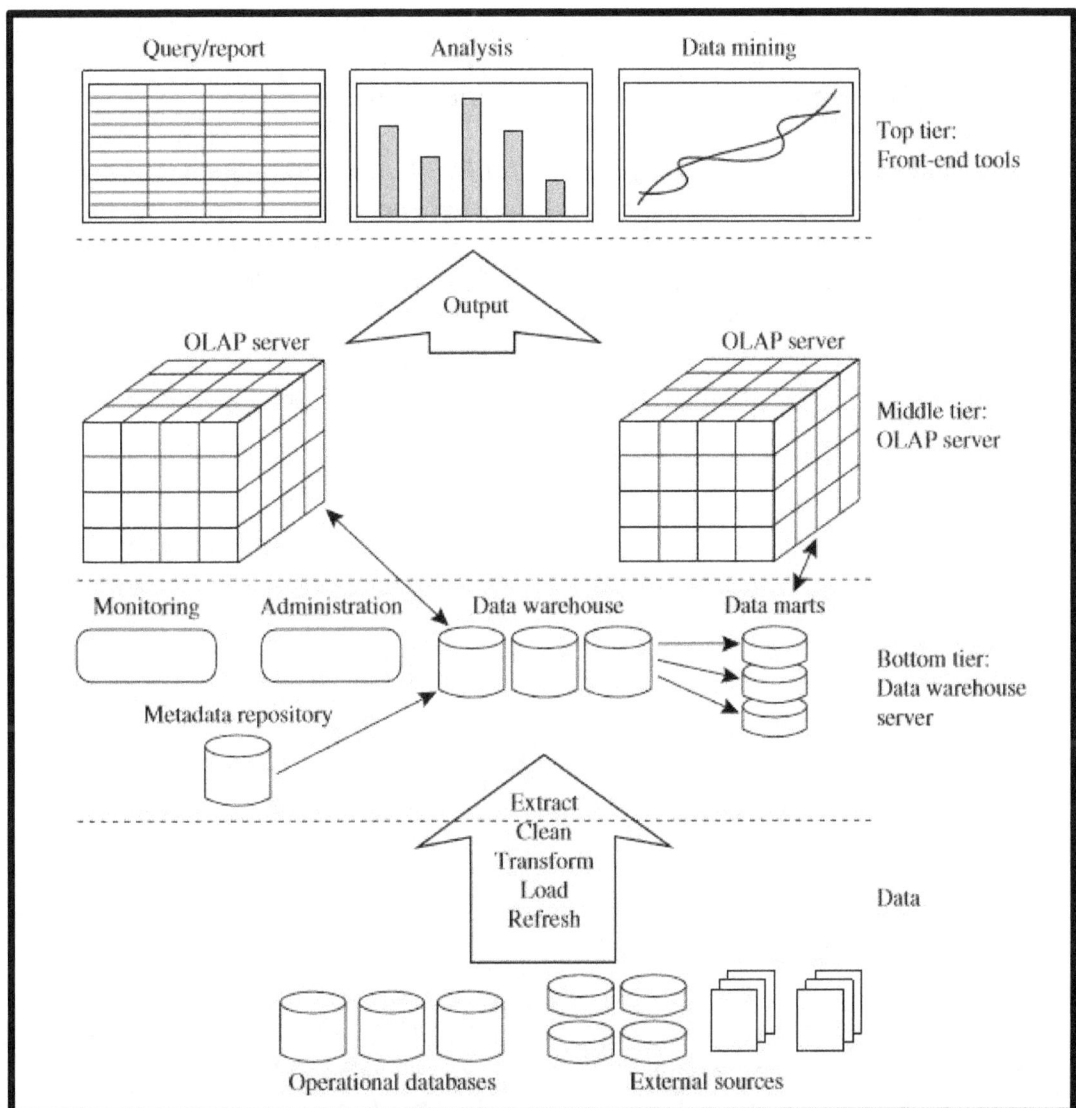

Figure 1: 3-Tier Data Warehouse Architecture

Generally, a **data warehouse** adopts a **three-tier architecture**. Following are the three tiers of the data warehouse architecture.

- **<u>Bottom Tier</u>** - The bottom tier of the architecture is the **data warehouse database server**. It is the **relational database system**. We use the back-end tools and utilities to feed data into the bottom tier from operational databases or other external sources. These back-end tools and utilities perform the **Extract, Clean, Load, & refresh** functions. The data is extracted using APIs known as **gateways**. A **gateway** is supported by the **underlying DBMS** and allows client programs to generate **SQL code to be executed** at a server. Examples of gateways include **ODBC (Open Database Connection)** and **OLEDB (Open Linking and Embedding for Databases)** by Microsoft and **JDBC (Java Database Connection)**. This tier also contains a **metadata repository**, which stores **information about the data warehouse and its contents**.

- <u>**Middle Tier**</u> - In the middle tier, we have the **OLAP Server** that can be implemented in either of the following ways.

  - By **Relational Online Analytical Processing (ROLAP)**, which is an **extended relational database management system**. The ROLAP maps the **operations on multidimensional data to standard relational operations**.

  - By **Multidimensional Online Analytical Processing (MOLAP)** model, which **directly implements the multidimensional data and operations**.

- <u>**Top-Tier**</u> - This tier is the **front-end client layer**. This layer holds the **query tools and reporting tools, analysis tools & data mining tools**.

Q2. Explain the Data Warehouse Models – Datamart, Enterprise Warehouse & Virtual Warehouse.

From the architecture point of view, there are three **data warehouse models**:

1. **Enterprise Warehouse**: An enterprise warehouse collects all of the information about subjects **spanning the entire organization**. It provides **corporate-wide data integration**, usually from one or more operational systems or external information providers, and is **cross-functional** in scope. It typically contains detailed data as well as summarized data, It can range in size from a few gigabytes to hundreds of gigabytes, terabytes, or beyond.

2. **Datamart**: A Datamart contains a **subset of corporate-wide data** that is of value to a **specific group of users**. We can claim that data marts contain data specific to a particular group. For example, the marketing data mart may contain data related to items, customers, and sales.

3. **Virtual Warehouse**: A virtual warehouse is a **set of views** over operational databases. It is easy to build a virtual warehouse. Building a virtual warehouse requires excess capacity on operational database servers.

Q3. What is OLAP? Mention the types of OLAPs – ROLAP, MOLAP & HOLAP.

Online Analytical Processing (OLAP) system is based on the **multidimensional data model**. It allows managers, and analysts to **get an insight of the information** through **fast, consistent, and interactive access to information**.

Types of OLAP Servers:

We have **four types of OLAP** servers:

1. **Relational OLAP (ROLAP)**
2. **Multidimensional OLAP (MOLAP)**
3. **Hybrid OLAP (HOLAP)**
4. **Specialized SQL Servers**

Relational OLAP (ROLAP):

ROLAP servers are placed between relational back-end server and client front-end tools. To store and manage warehouse data, ROLAP uses relational or extended-relational DBMS. The ROLAP maps the operations on multidimensional data to standard relational operations.

Multidimensional OLAP (MOLAP):

MOLAP uses array-based multidimensional storage engines for multidimensional views of data. It directly implements the multidimensional data and operations. With multidimensional data stores, the storage utilization may be low if the data set is sparse. Therefore, many MOLAP server use two levels of data storage representation to handle dense and sparse data sets.

Hybrid OLAP (HOLAP):

Hybrid OLAP is a combination of both ROLAP and MOLAP. It offers higher scalability of ROLAP and faster computation of MOLAP. HOLAP servers allows to store the large data volumes of detailed information. The aggregations are stored separately in MOLAP store.

Specialized SQL Servers:

Specialized SQL servers provide advanced query language and query processing support for SQL queries over star and snowflake schemas in a read-only environment.

Q4. OLAP vs OLTP:

Sr. No.	Online Analytical Processing (OLAP) {Data Warehouses}	Online Transaction Processing (OLTP) {Operational Database Systems}
1	**Data Warehouse** systems serve users in the role of **data analysis & decision making**. These systems are known as **Online Analytical Processing (OLAP)** systems.	**Online Operational Database Systems** performs **online transaction & query processing**. These systems are called **Online Transaction Processing (OLTP)** systems.
2	Involves **historical processing** of information.	Involves **day-to-day processing** of information.
3	OLAP systems are used by **knowledge workers** such as executives, managers and analysts.	OLTP systems are used by **clerks, DBAs, or database professionals**.
4	Useful in **analyzing the business**.	Useful in **running the business**.
5	It focuses on **Information out**.	It focuses on **Data in**.
6	Based on **Star Schema, Snowflake Schema & Fact Constellation Schema**.	Based on **Entity Relationship Model**.
7	OLAP adopts a **subject-oriented database design**.	OLTP adopts an **application-oriented database design**.
8	Contains **historical data**.	Contains **current data**.
9	Provides **summarized and consolidated (combined) data**.	Provides **primitive (raw) and highly detailed data**.
10	Provides **summarized & multidimensional view of data**.	Provides **detailed & flat relational view of data**.
11	Number of **users** is in **hundreds**.	Number of **users** is in **thousands**.
12	Number of **records accessed** is in **millions**.	Number of **records accessed** is in **tens**.
13	**Database size** is from **100 GB to 1 TB**	**Database size** is from **100 MB to 1 GB**.
14	**Highly flexible**.	Provides **high performance**.

Q5. Explain Data Cube & Cuboid.

A **data cube** allows data to be modeled and viewed in multiple dimensions. It is defined by **dimensions and facts**.

- o **Dimensions** are the perspectives or entities with respect to which an organization wants to keep records. For example, General Electronics may create a sales data warehouse in order to keep records of the company's sales with respect to the dimensions: time, item, branch, and location. Each dimension may have a table associated with it, called a dimension table, which further describes the dimension. For example, a dimension table for item may contain the attributes item name, brand, and type.

- o A multidimensional data model is typically organized around a central theme, such as sales. This theme is represented by a fact table. **Facts** are numeric measures. Examples of facts for a sales data warehouse include dollars sold (sales amount in dollars), units sold (number of units sold), and amount budgeted. The fact table contains the names of the facts as well as keys to each of the related dimension tables.

Although we usually think of cubes as 3-D geometric structures, in data warehousing **the data cube is n-dimensional**.

Consider the following sales data with three dimensions: time, item & location, for the cities Chicago, New York, Toronto, and Vancouver.

	location = "Chicago"				location = "New York"				location = "Toronto"				location = "Vancouver"			
	item				item				item				item			
time	home ent.	comp.	phone	sec.	home ent.	comp.	phone	sec.	home ent.	comp.	phone	sec.	home ent.	comp.	phone	sec.
Q1	854	882	89	623	1087	968	38	872	818	746	43	591	605	825	14	400
Q2	943	890	64	698	1130	1024	41	925	894	769	52	682	680	952	31	512
Q3	1032	924	59	789	1034	1048	45	1002	940	795	58	728	812	1023	30	501
Q4	1129	992	63	870	1142	1091	54	984	978	864	59	784	927	1038	38	580

Note: The measure displayed is *dollars_sold* (in thousands).

The **3-D data** in the table are represented as a **series of 2-D tables**. Conceptually, we may also represent the same data in the form of a **3-D data cube**, as in the following figure:

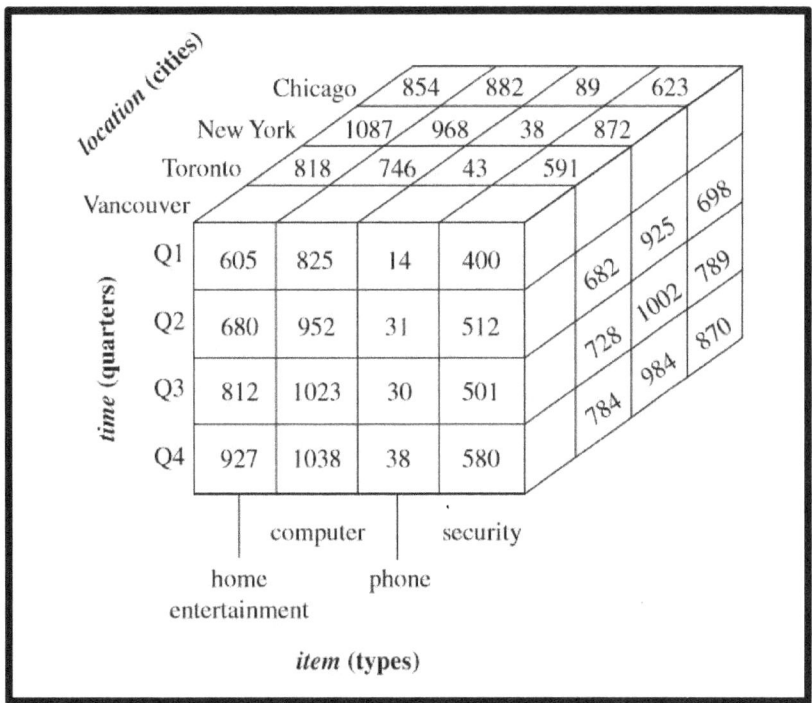

Figure 2: Data Cube

In the data warehousing literature, a ***data cube*** like shown in the above figure is often referred to as a ***cuboid***. Given a set of dimensions, we can generate a ***cuboid for each of the possible subsets of the given dimensions***. The result would form ***a lattice (network) of cuboids***, each showing the data at a different level of summarization, or group-by.

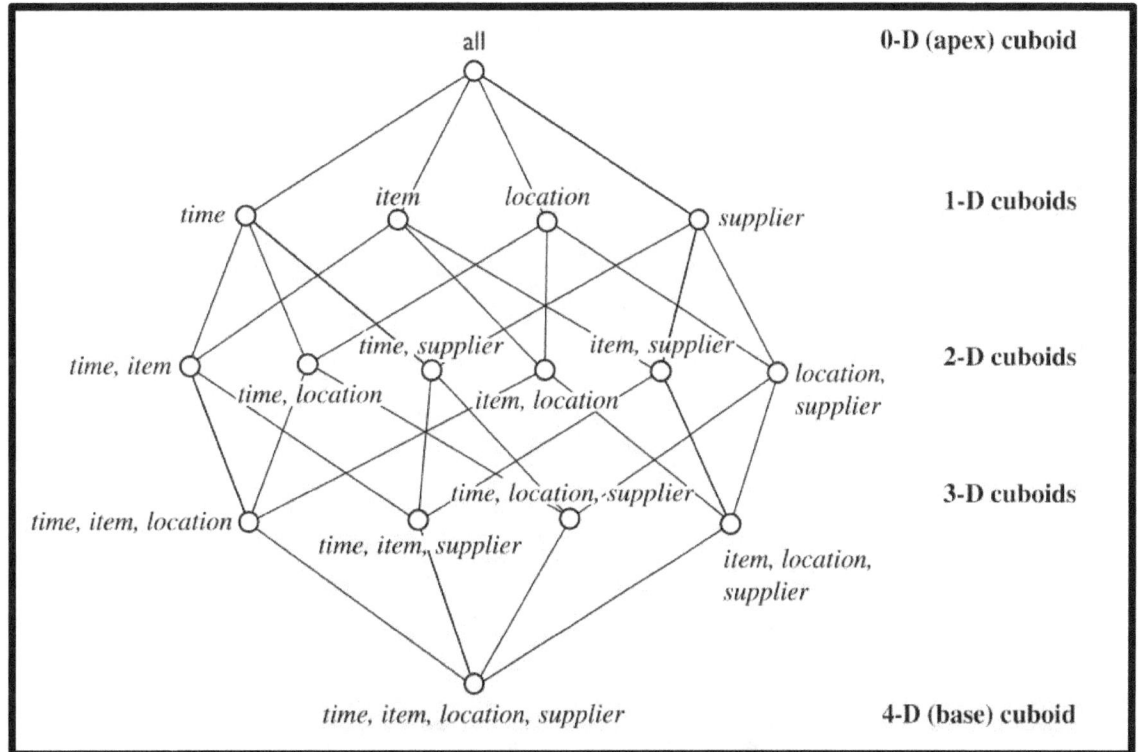

Figure 3: Data Cube - Lattice Structure

The 0-D cuboid, which holds the highest level of summarization, is called the ***apex cuboid***.

The 4-D cuboid, which holds the lowest level of summarization is called the ***base cuboid***.

Q6. Illustrate the OLAP operations on data cube- drill down, Roll Up, Pivot, Slice & Dice.

Since **OLAP servers** are based on **multidimensional view** of data, we will discuss OLAP operations in multidimensional data.

Here is the list of **OLAP operations**:

- o **Roll-up**
- o **Drill-down**
- o **Slice and dice**
- o **Pivot (rotate)**

Roll-up:

Roll-up performs **aggregation on a data cube** in any of the following ways:

- o **By climbing up a concept hierarchy for a dimension**
- o **By dimension reduction**

The following diagram illustrates how roll-up works:

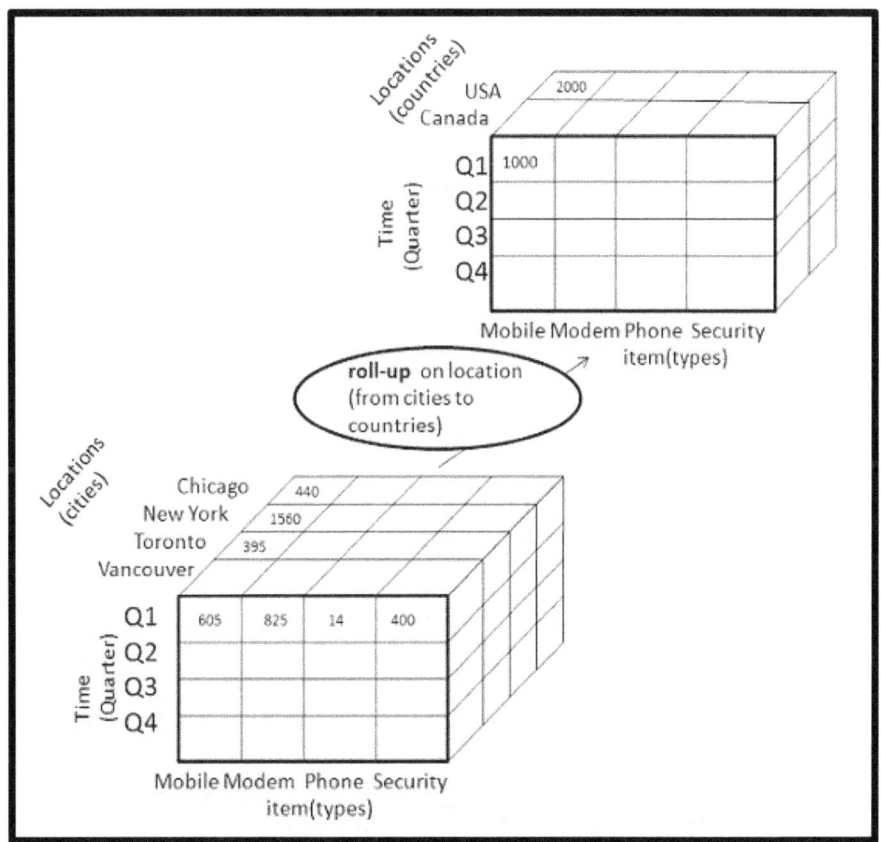

Figure 4: OLAP Operation Roll-up

- o **Roll-up** is performed by ***climbing up a concept hierarchy*** for the dimension *'location'*.

- o Initially the concept hierarchy was ***"street < city < province < country"***.

- o On rolling up, the data is aggregated by ***ascending the location hierarchy*** from the ***level of city*** to the ***level of country***.

- o When roll-up is performed, one or more ***dimensions*** from the data cube are ***removed***.

Drill-down:

Drill-down is the ***reverse operation of roll-up***. It is performed by either of the following ways:

- ***By stepping down a concept hierarchy for a dimension***
- ***By introducing a new dimension.***

The following diagram illustrates how drill-down works:

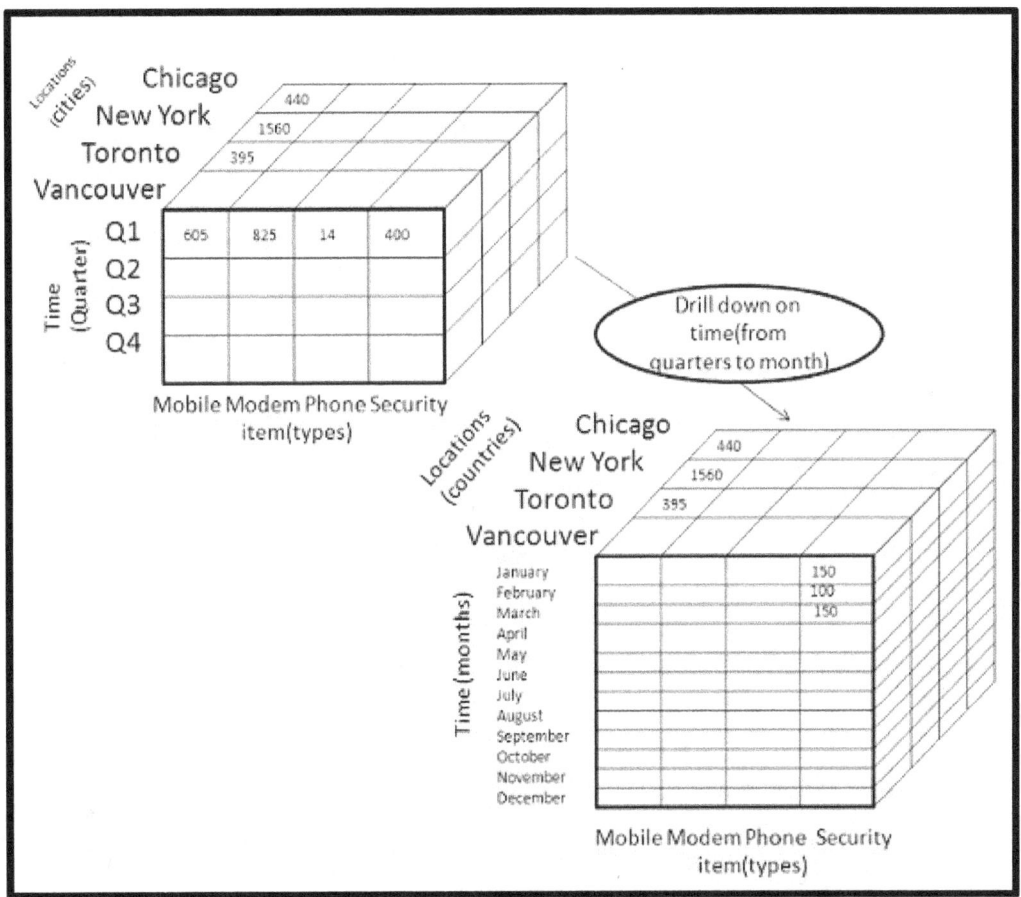

Figure 5: OLAP Operation Drill-down

- ***Drill-down*** is performed by ***stepping down a concept hierarchy*** for the dimension '***time***'.

- Initially the concept hierarchy was ***"day < month < quarter < year"***.

- On drilling down, the ***time dimension is descended*** from the ***level of quarter*** to the ***level of month***.

- When drill-down is performed, one or more ***dimensions*** to the data cube are ***added***.

- It navigates from ***less detailed data*** to ***highly detailed data***.

Slice:

The slice operation *selects one particular dimension* from a given cube & *provides a new sub-cube*.

Consider the following diagram that shows how slice works.

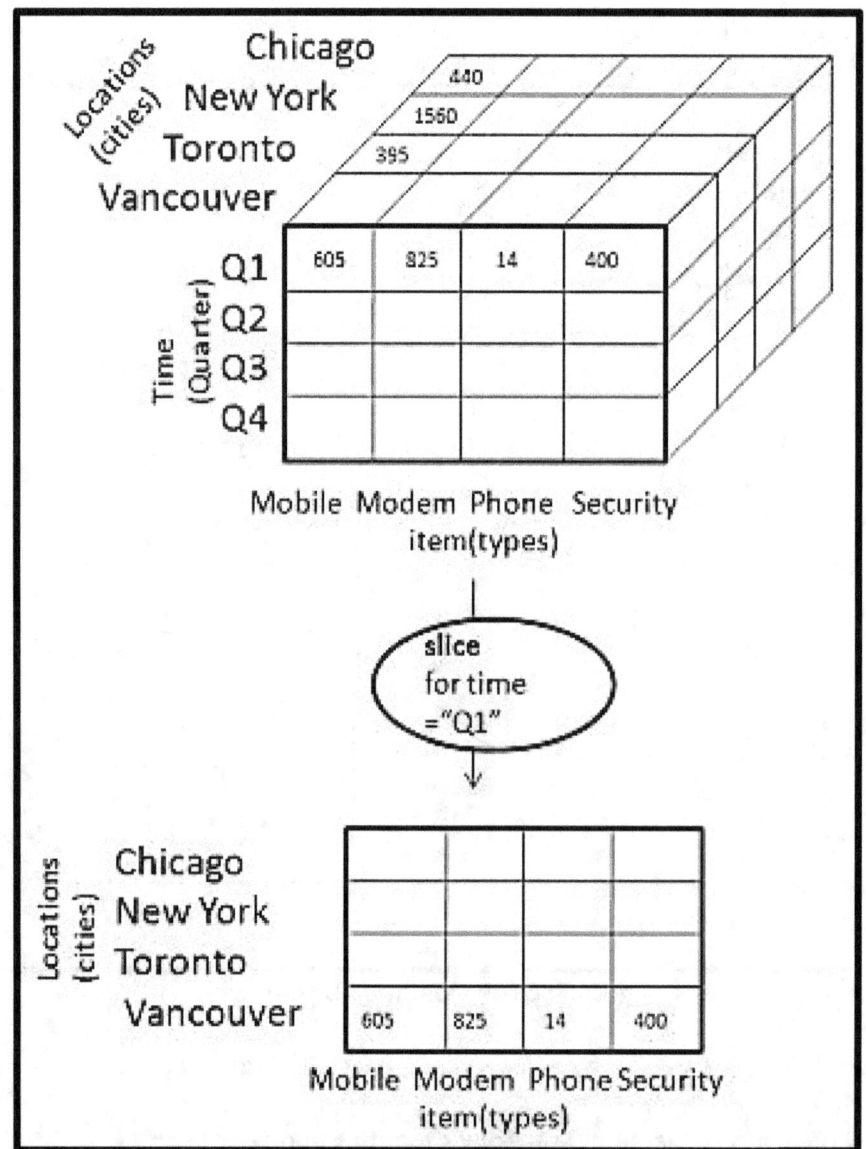

Figure 6: OLAP Operation Slice

o　Here, *Slice* is performed for the *dimension "time"* using the *criterion time = "Q1"*.

o　It will form a *new sub-cube* by selecting the two dimensions: *"location" & "item"*.

Dice:

Dice **selects two or more dimensions** from a given cube and **provides a new sub-cube**.

Consider the following diagram that shows the dice operation.

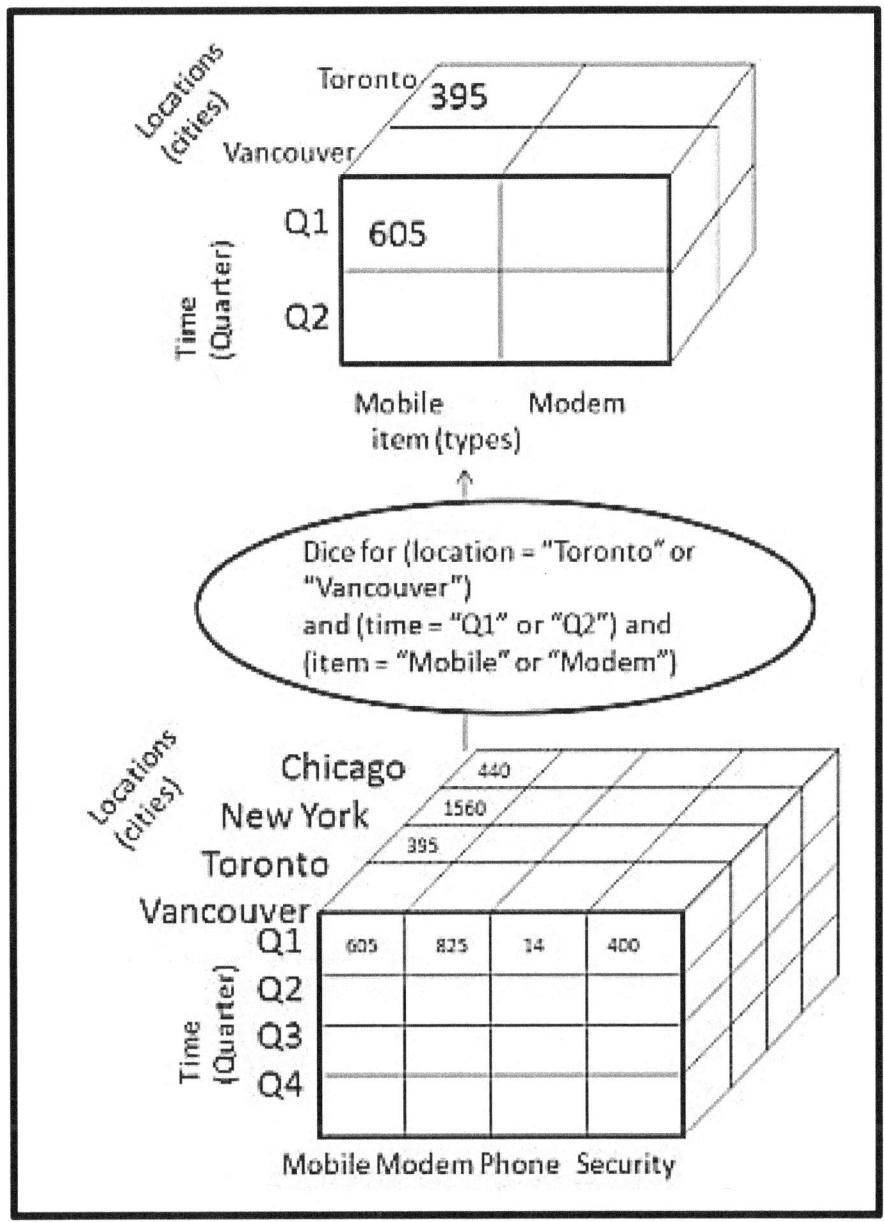

Figure 7: OLAP Operation Dice

The **dice operation on the above cube** is based on the **following selection criteria** that involves **three dimensions**.

1. *(location = "Toronto" or "Vancouver")*
2. *(time = "Q1" or "Q2")*
3. *(item =" Mobile" or "Modem")*

Pivot:

The *pivot* operation is *also known as rotation*. It *rotates the data axis* in view in order *to provide an alternative presentation of data*.

Consider the following diagram that shows the pivot operation.

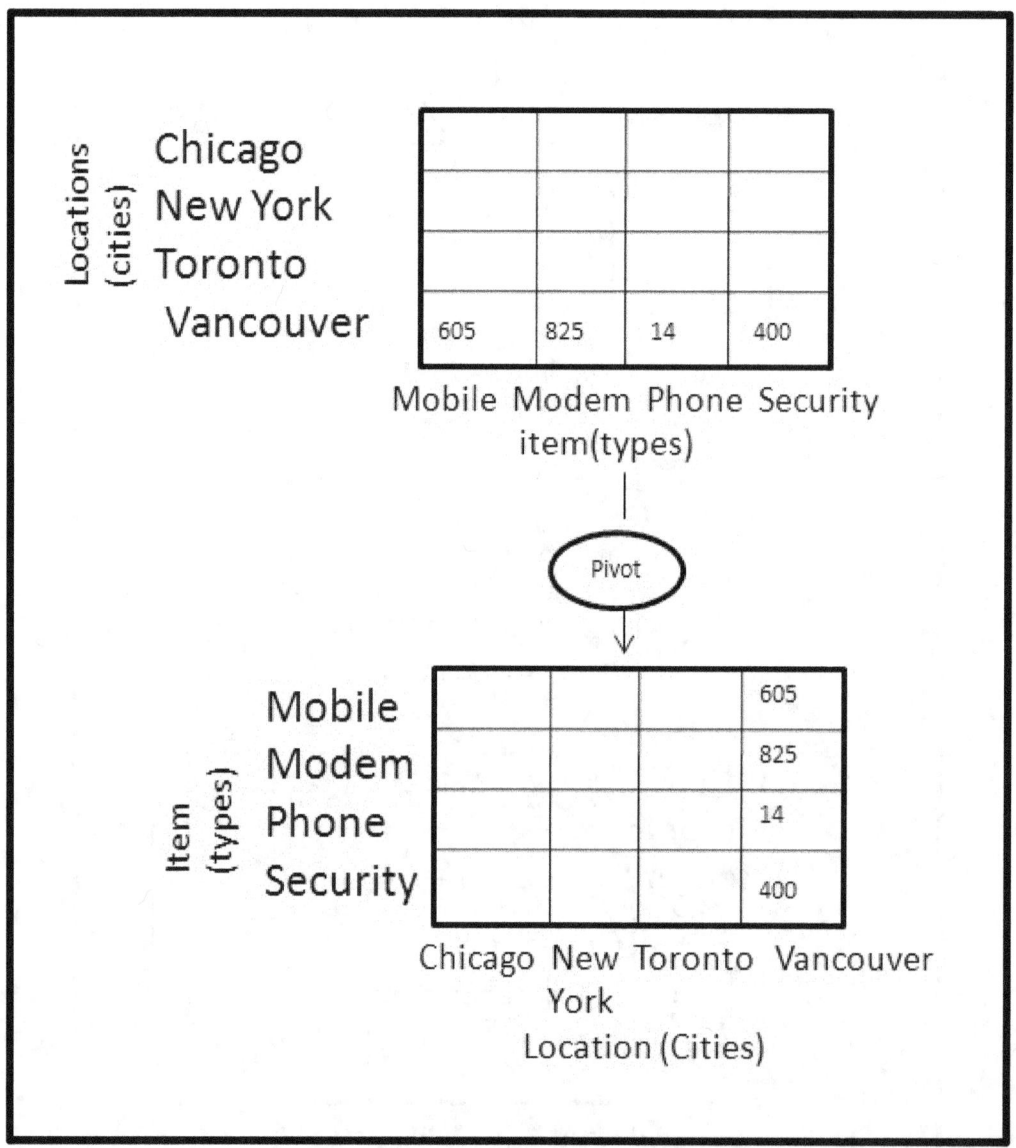

Figure 8: OLAP Operation Pivot

In the above figure, the *item & location axes*, in 2-D slice, *are rotated*.

Q7. Starting with the base cuboid [day, doctor, patient], what specific OLAP operations should be performed in order to list the total fee collected by each doctor in 2004?

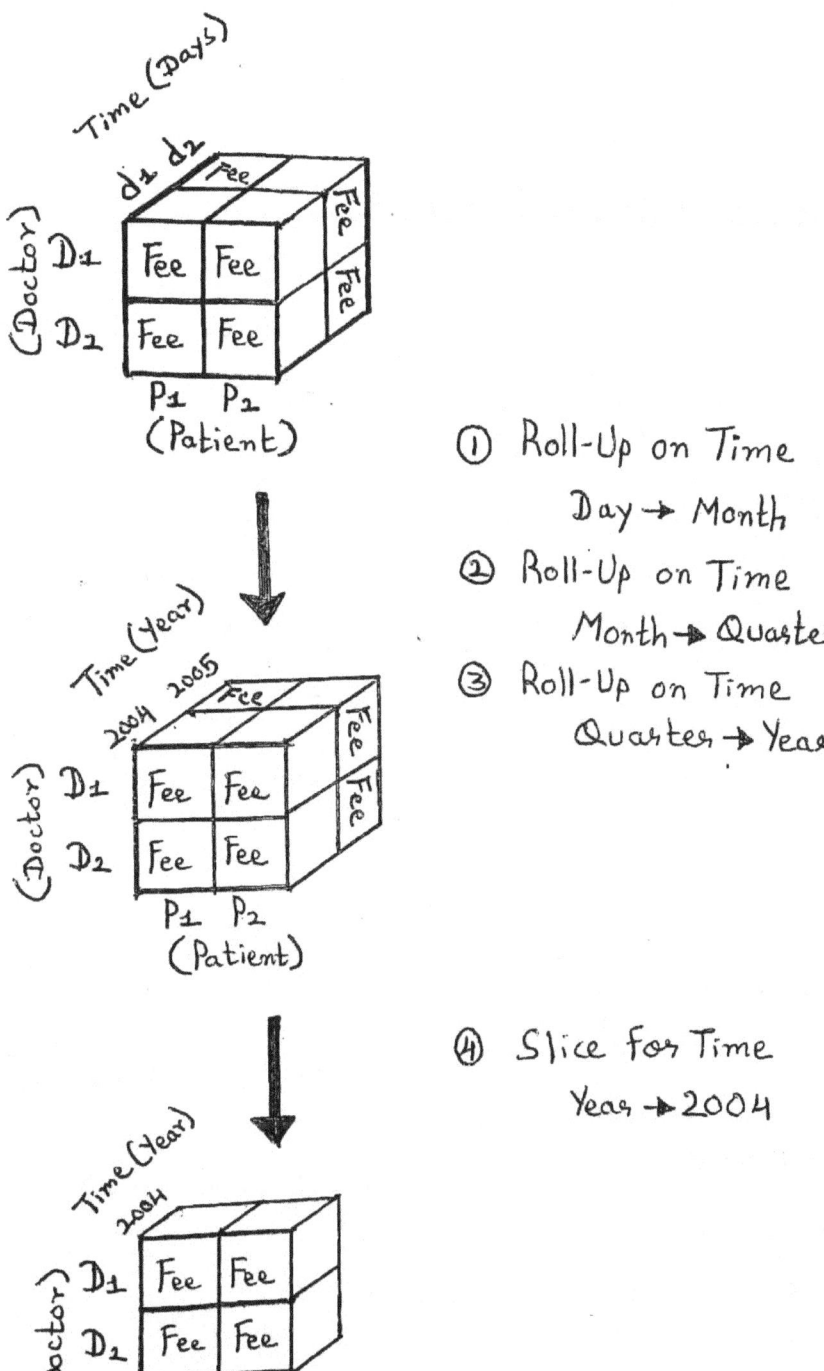

① Roll-Up on Time
   Day → Month
② Roll-Up on Time
   Month → Quarter
③ Roll-Up on Time
   Quarter → Year

④ Slice for Time
   Year → 2004

Q8. What do you mean by data mart? What are the different types of data mart?

Data Marts contain a **subset of organization-wide data** that is valuable to specific groups of people in an organization. A data mart contains only those data that is **specific to a particular group**.

Data marts improve end-user response time by allowing users to have access only to the specific type of data they need to view.

A **data mart** is basically a **condensed and more focused version of a data warehouse** that reflects the **regulations of each business unit within an organization**. Each **data mart** is **dedicated to a specific business function**. Data marts are confined to subjects.

For **example**, the marketing data mart may contain only data related to items, customers, and sales.

Reasons to create a data mart:

- o   To partition data in order to **impose access control strategies**.

- o   To speed up the queries by **reducing the volume of data to be scanned**.

- o   To **segment data into different hardware platforms**.

- o   To **structure data** in a form suitable **for a user access** tool.

- o   To lower the cost of implementing a full data warehouse.

Types of data marts:

Three basic types of data marts are dependent, independent, and hybrid. The categorization is based primarily on the data source that feeds the data mart.

- o   Dependent data marts draw data from a central data warehouse that has already been created.

- o   Independent data marts are standalone systems built by drawing data directly from operational or external sources of data or both.

- o   Hybrid data marts can draw data from operational systems or data warehouses.

1. Dependent Data Marts:

o   A dependent data mart allows you to unite your organization's data in one data warehouse.

o   This gives you the usual advantages of centralization.

o   This kind of data marts draws data from a central data warehouse that has already been created.

o   The following figure illustrates a dependent data mart.

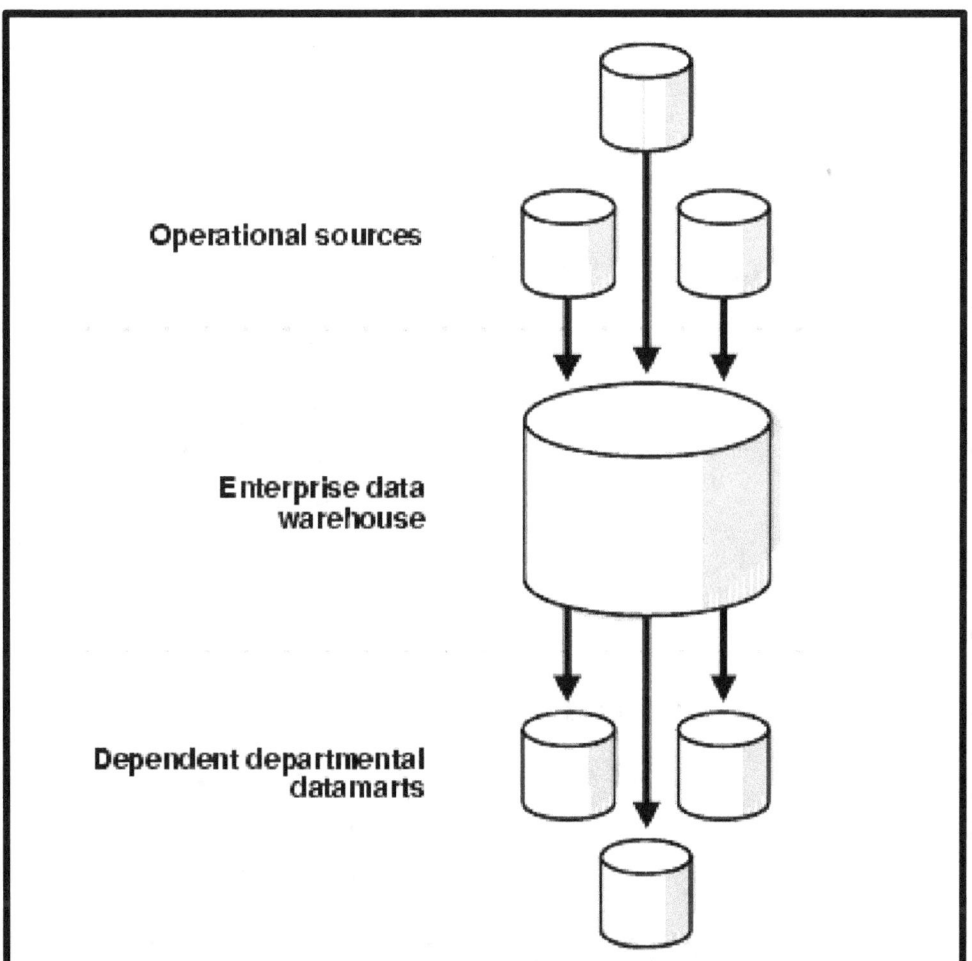

Figure 9: Dependent Data Marts

2. Independent Data Marts:

o   An independent data mart is created without the use of a central data warehouse.

o   This kind of data marts draws data directly from operational or external sources of data or both.

o   This could be desirable for smaller groups within an organization.

o   The following figure illustrates an independent data mart.

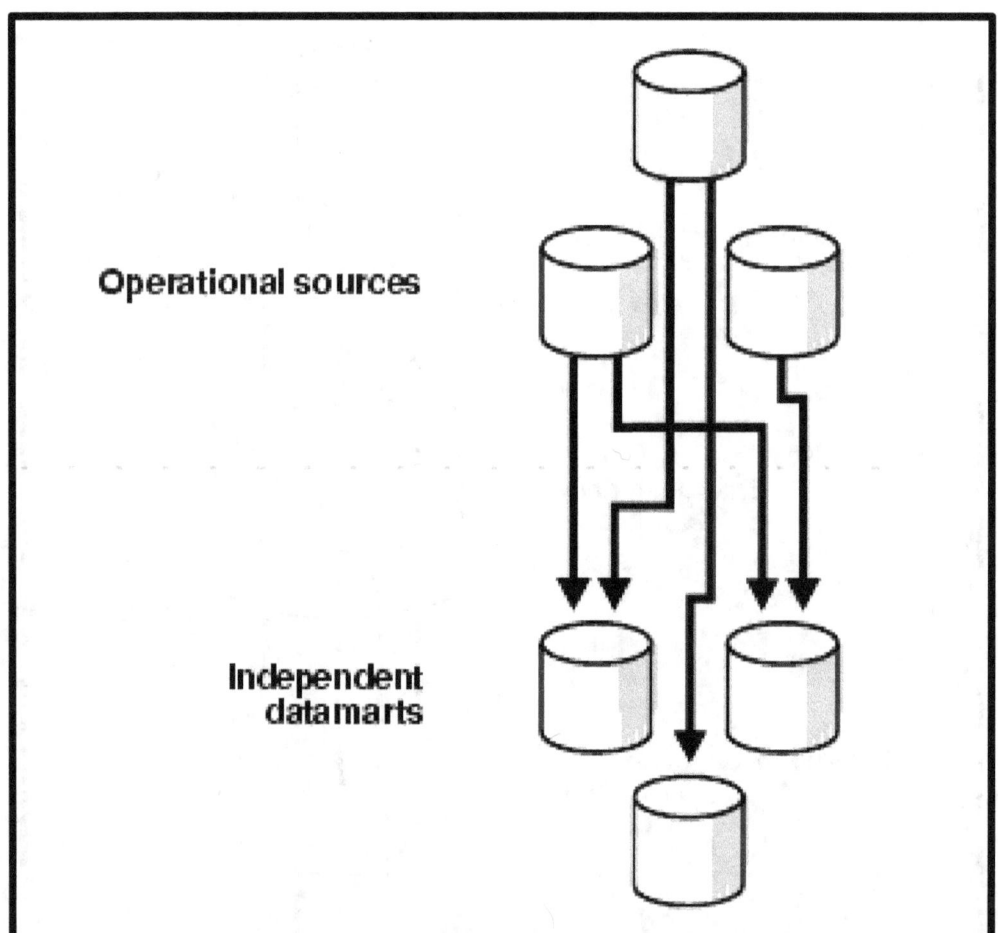

Figure 10: Independent Data Marts

3. Hybrid Data Marts:

o   A hybrid data mart allows you to combine input from sources other than a data warehouse.

o   This kind of data marts can draw data from operational systems as well as data warehouses.

o   This could be useful for many situations, especially when you need ad hoc integration, probably after a new group or product is added to the organization.

o   The following figure illustrates a hybrid data mart.

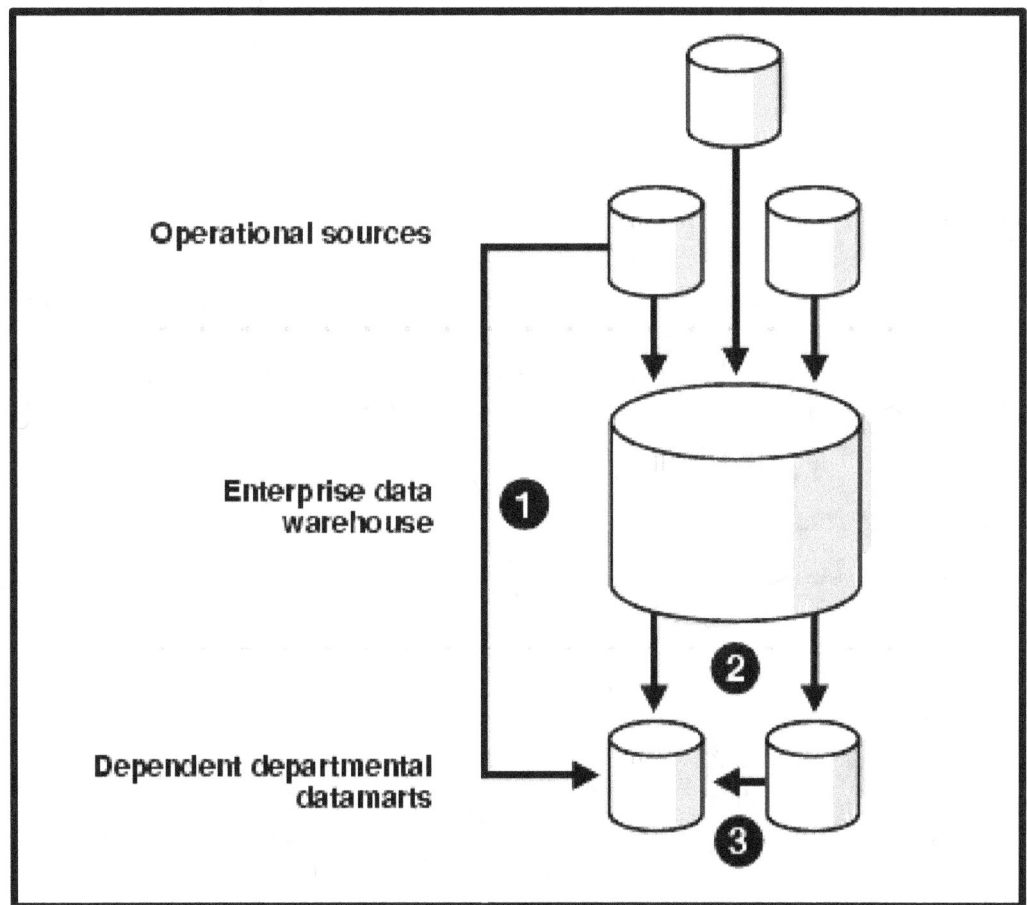

Figure 11: Hybrid Data Marts

Q9. Explain Star, Snowflake, and Fact Constellation Schema for Multidimensional Database.

Schema is a *logical description of the entire database*. It includes the *name and description of records* of all record types including all *associated data-items & aggregates*.

The *Entity-Relationship data model* is commonly used in the design of *relational databases*, where a *database schema* consists of a set of *entities and the relationships between them*. Such a data model is appropriate for *Online Transaction Processing (OLTP)*.

A *Data Warehouse*, however, requires a concise, *subject-oriented schema* that facilitates *Online Analytical Processing (OLAP)*. The most popular data model for a data warehouse is a *multidimensional model*. Such a model can exist in the form of a *Star Schema*, *a Snowflake Schema*, or *a Fact Constellation Schema*.

Star Schema:

The most common modeling paradigm is the *star schema*, in which the *data warehouse contains*:

1. *A large central table (fact table) containing the bulk of the data, with no redundancy, and*
2. *A set of smaller attendant tables (dimension tables), one for each dimension.*

The *schema graph* resembles a *starburst*, with the *dimension tables* displayed in a *radial pattern around the central fact table*.

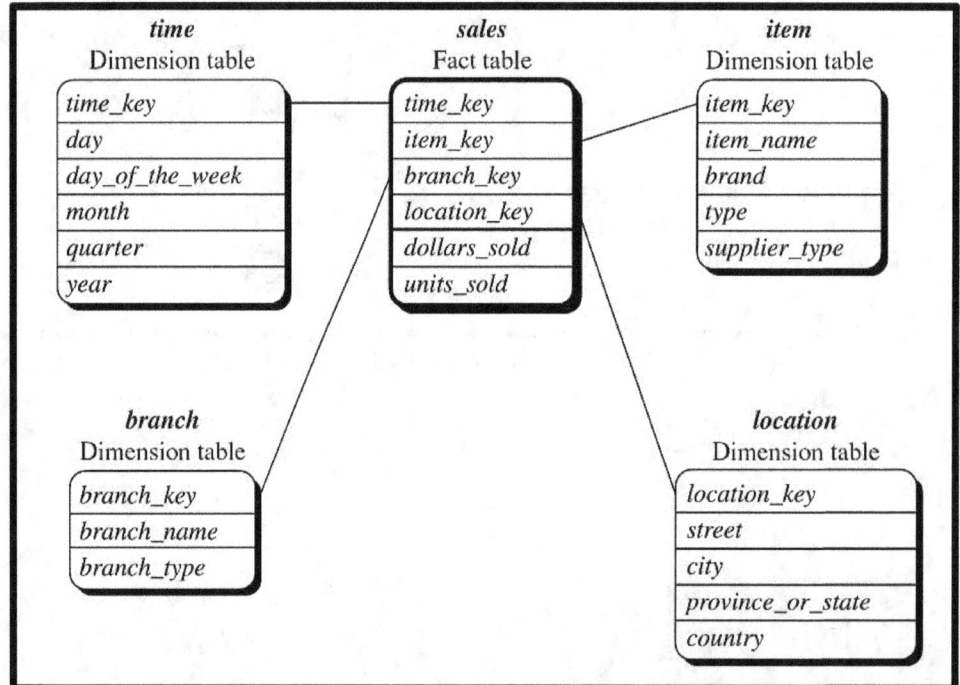

Figure 12: Star Schema for Multidimensional Database

Notice that in the **star schema**, **each dimension** is represented by **only one table**, and **each table** contains a **set of attributes**. For example, the **location dimension table** contains the attribute set **{location key, street, city, province or state, country}**. This constraint may introduce some **redundancy**. For example, **"Vancouver"** and **"Victoria"** both the cities are in the **Canadian province of British Columbia**. The entries for such cities may cause **data redundancy** along the attributes **province or state** and **country**.

Snowflake Schema:

The **snowflake schema** is a **variant of the star schema** model, where some **dimension tables are normalized**, thereby further splitting the data into **additional tables**. The resulting schema graph forms a **shape similar to a snowflake**.

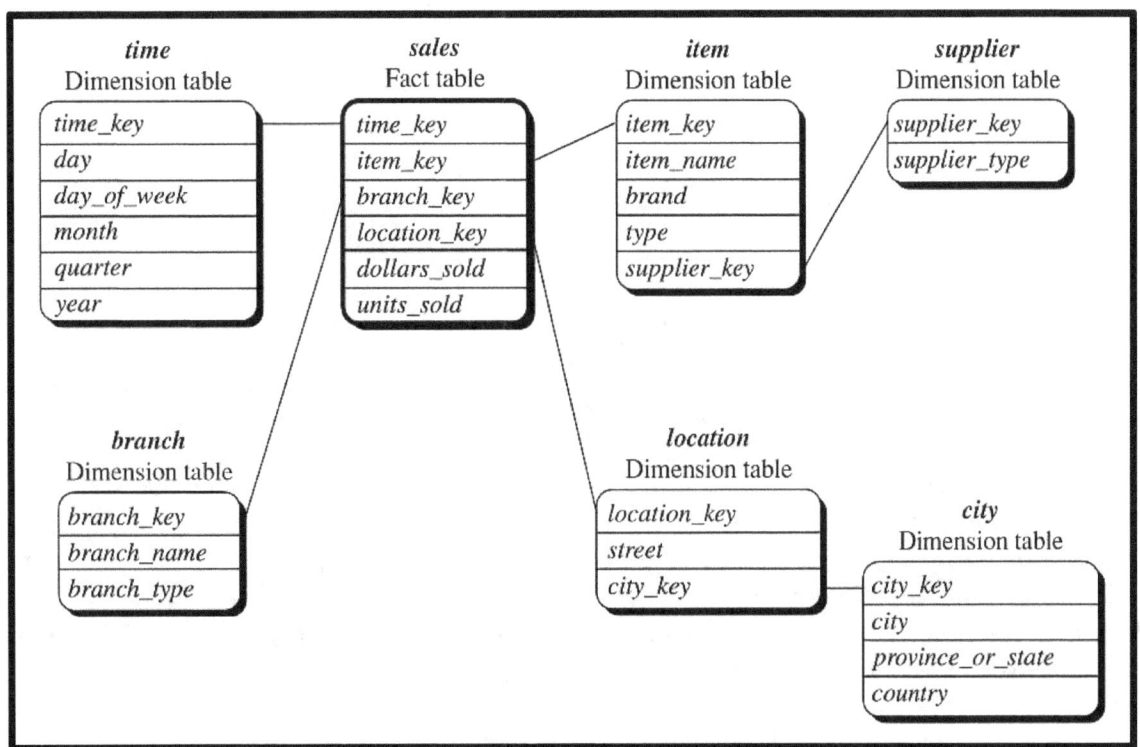

Figure 13: Snowflake Schema for Multidimensional Database

Unlike Star schema, the **dimension tables** in a snowflake schema are **normalized**. For example, the **item dimension table** in star schema is **normalized** and split **into two dimension tables**, namely **item table** and **supplier table**. Due to normalization, the **redundancy is reduced** and therefore, it becomes easy to maintain and the **save storage space**.

However, this **space savings is negligible** in comparison to the **magnitude of the fact table**. Furthermore, the snowflake structure can **reduce the effectiveness of browsing**, since more joins will be needed to execute a query. Consequently, the **system performance** may be **adversely impacted**.

Fact Constellation Schema:

Sophisticated applications may require *multiple fact tables* to *share dimension tables*. This kind of schema can be viewed as a *collection of stars*, and hence is called a *Galaxy Schema* or a *Fact Constellation*.

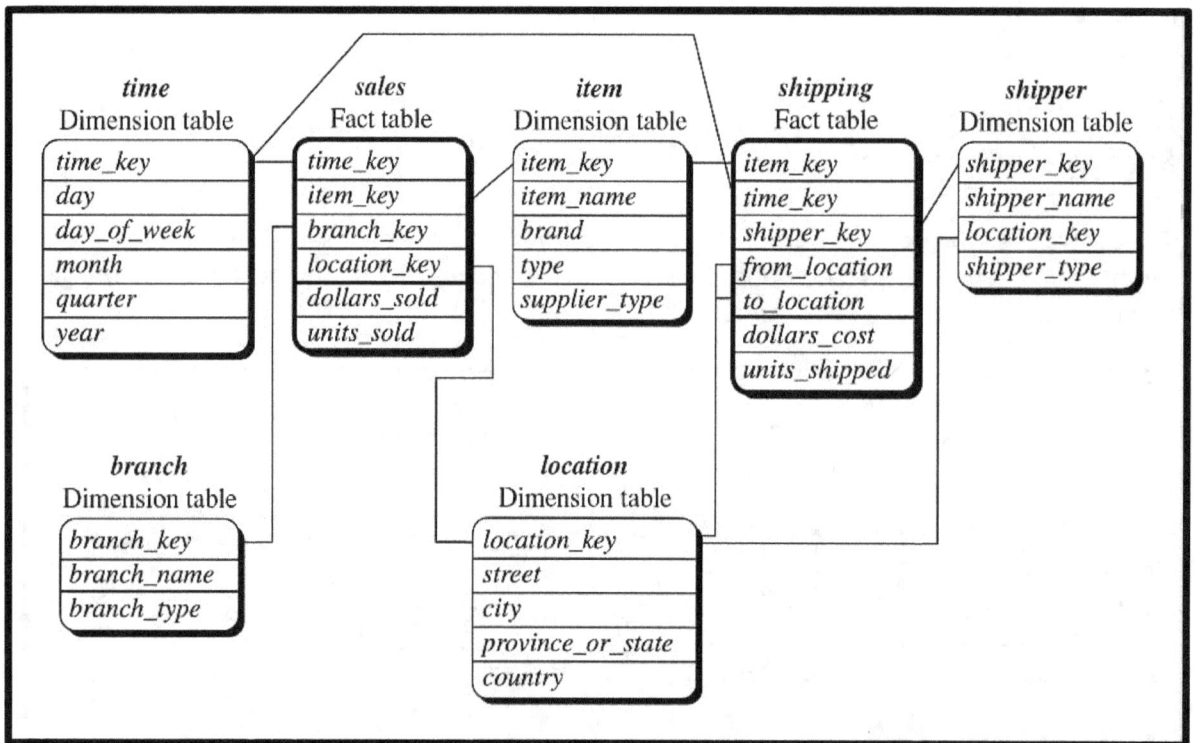

Figure 14: Fact Constellation Schema for Multidimensional Database

A *fact constellation* schema is shown in the above Figure. This schema specifies *two fact tables*, *sales & shipping*. The sales table definition is identical to that of the star schema. The shipping table has five dimensions — *item key, time key, shipper key, from location, & to location* — and two measures—*dollars cost & units shipped*. A fact constellation schema allows *dimension tables to be shared between fact tables*. For example, the dimension tables for *time, item, and location* are *shared between the sales and shipping fact tables*.

In data warehousing, there is a distinction between a *Data Warehouse* & a *Datamart*.

A *Data Warehouse* collects information about subjects that span the entire organization and thus its scope is *enterprise-wide*. For Data Warehouses, the *fact constellation schema* is commonly used, since it can model multiple, interrelated subjects.

A *Datamart*, on the other hand, is a department subset of the Data Warehouse that focuses on selected subjects, and thus its scope is *department-wide*. For data marts, *the star or snowflake schema* is commonly used, since both are geared toward modeling single subjects.

Q10. Explain Fact table vs. Dimension table with neat diagram.

Basis for Comparison	Fact Table	Dimension Table
Basic	Fact table contains the measurement & the attributes of a dimension table.	Dimension table contains the attributes along which fact table calculates the metric.
Attribute & Records	Fact table contains less attributes and more records.	Dimension table contains more attributes and less records.
Table size	Fact table grows Vertically.	Dimension table grows horizontally.
Key	Fact table contains a primary key which is a concatenation of primary keys of all dimension table.	Each dimension table contains its primary key.
Creation	Fact table can be created only when dimension tables are completely created.	Dimension tables need to be created before the fact table is created.
Schema	A schema contains less number of fact tables.	A schema contains more number of dimension tables.
Format of Attributes	Fact table can have data in numeric as well as textual format.	Dimension table always contains attributes in textual format.

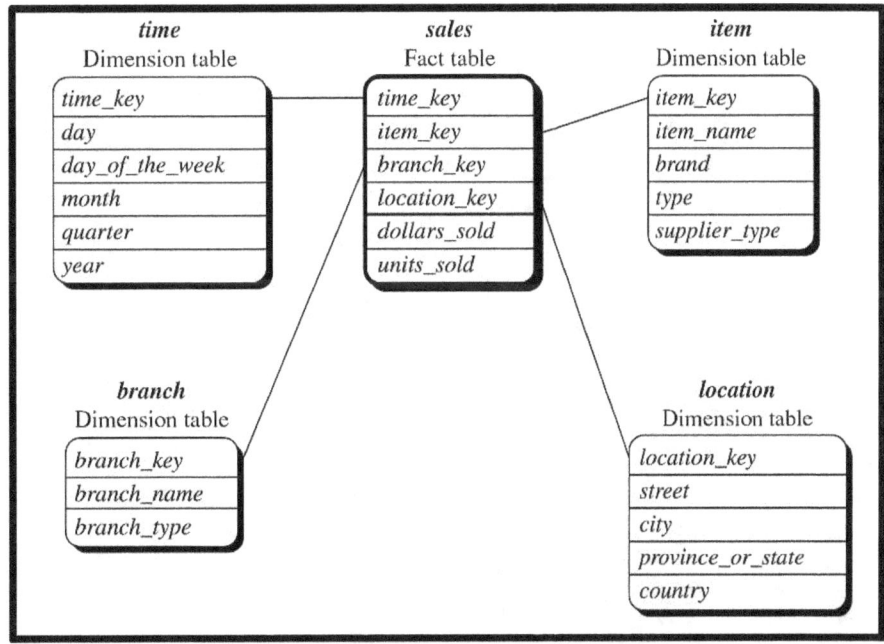

Figure 15: Fact Table vs Dimension Table

Q11. Define following terms: Data Mart, Enterprise Warehouse & Virtual Warehouse.

Refer
to
PAGE 6
Of
This
book.

Q12. Draw and explain the data mining architecture.

The fast-growing, tremendous amount of data, collected and stored in large data repositories, has far exceeded our human ability for comprehension without powerful tools. As a result, data collected in large data repositories become *"data tombs"* — *data archives that are seldom visited*.

There is a *huge amount of data available* in the Information Industry. This data is of *no use until it is converted into useful information*. It is necessary to *analyze this huge amount of data and extract useful information from it*. This is where *data mining* comes in to the picture.

Data Mining is defined as *extraction of information* from *huge sets of data*. In other words, we can say that data mining is the procedure of *mining knowledge from data*.

Data Mining Architecture:

The major components of any data mining system are data source, data warehouse server, data mining engine, pattern evaluation module, graphical user interface and knowledge base.

o **Data Sources**: Database, data warehouse, World Wide Web (WWW), text files and other documents are the actual sources of data. You need large volumes of historical data for data mining to be successful. Organizations usually store data in databases or data warehouses. Data warehouses may contain one or more databases, text files, spreadsheets or other kinds of information repositories. Sometimes, data may reside even in plain text files or spreadsheets. World Wide Web or the Internet is another big source of data.

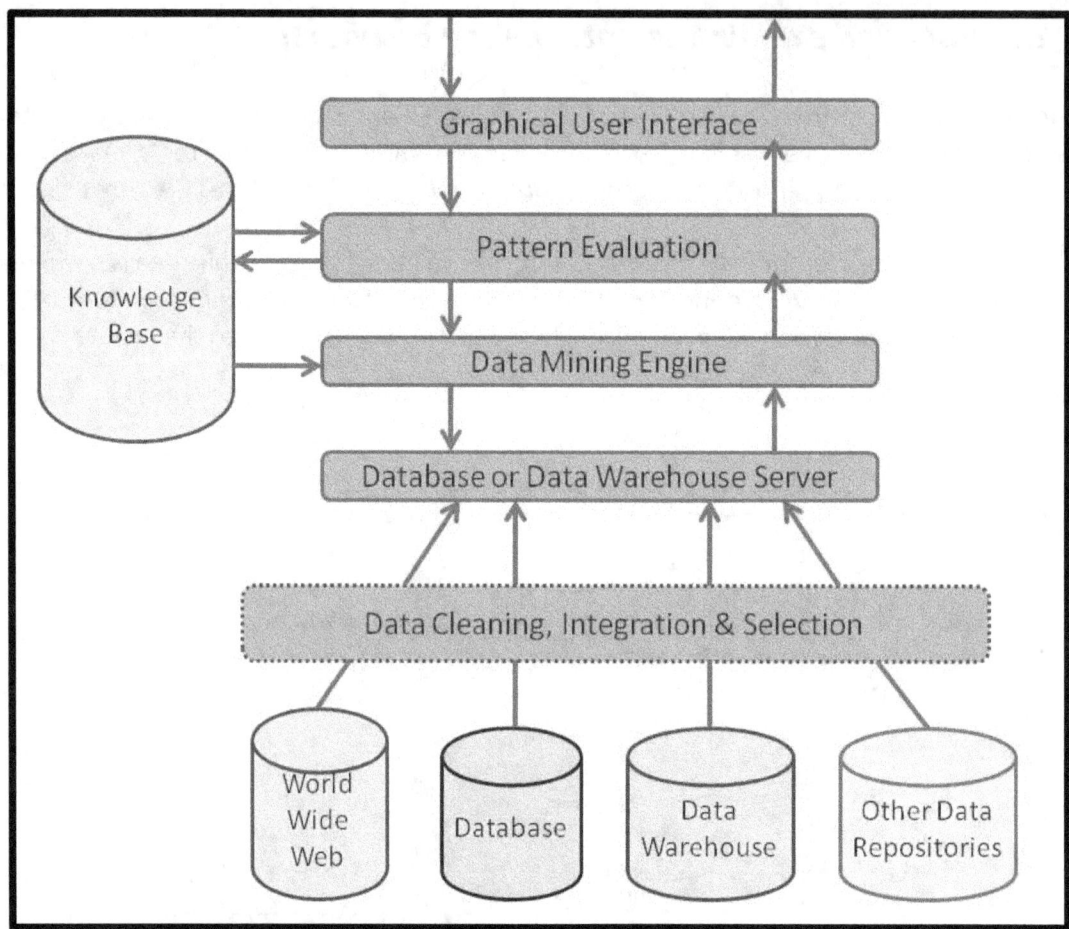

Figure 16: Data Mining Architecture

o **_Processing on Data from Data Sources_**: The data needs to be cleaned, integrated and selected before passing it to the data warehouse server. As the data is from different sources and in different formats, it cannot be used directly for the data mining process because the data might not be complete and reliable. So, first data needs to be cleaned and integrated.

o **_Data Warehouse Server_**: The database or data warehouse server contains the actual data that is ready to be processed. Hence, it is responsible for retrieving the relevant data based on the data mining request of the user.

o **_Data Mining Engine_**: The data mining engine is the core component of any data mining system. It consists of a number of modules for performing data mining tasks including association, classification, characterization, clustering, prediction, time-series analysis etc.

o **_Pattern Evaluation Modules_**: The pattern evaluation module is mainly responsible for the measure of interestingness of the data pattern by using a threshold value. It interacts with the data mining engine to focus the search towards interesting patterns.

o **_Graphical User Interface_**: The GUI module communicates between the user and the data mining system. This module helps the user to use the system easily and efficiently without knowing the real complexity behind the process. When the user specifies a query or a task, this module interacts with the data mining system and displays the result in an easily understandable manner.

- o **_Knowledge Base:_** The knowledge base is helpful in the whole data mining process. It might be useful for guiding the search or evaluating the interestingness of the result patterns. The knowledge base might even contain user beliefs and data from user experiences that can be useful in the process of data mining. The data mining engine might get inputs from the knowledge base to make the result more accurate and reliable. The pattern evaluation module interacts with the knowledge base on a regular basis to get inputs regarding the interestingness of the data patterns.

Q13. Explain KDD (Knowledge Discovery from Data) process in Data Mining.

Many people treat **data mining** as a synonym for the term, **knowledge discovery from data (KDD)**, while others view data mining as merely an essential step in the process of knowledge discovery.

KDD refers to the **overall process of discovering useful knowledge from data**. It involves the evaluation and possibly interpretation of the patterns to make the decision of what qualifies as knowledge. It also includes the choice of **encoding schemes, preprocessing, sampling, and projections of the data** prior to the data mining step.

While, **data m7ining** refers to the application of algorithms for **extracting patterns from data** without the additional steps of the KDD process.

Here is the **list of steps involved in the KDD process**:

1. **Data Preprocessing -** Databases are notoriously "noisy" or contain inaccurate or missing data. During the preprocessing stage the data is cleaned & is prepared for mining.

    a. **Data Cleaning** – In this step, the noise and inconsistent data is removed.

    b. **Data Integration** – In this step, multiple data sources are combined.

    c. **Data Selection** – In this step, data relevant to the analysis task are retrieved from the database.

2. **Data Transformation** – In this step, data is transformed or consolidated into forms appropriate for mining by performing summary or aggregation operations. This phase attempts to limit or reduce the number of data elements that are evaluated, while maintaining the validity of the data. During this stage data is organized, converted from one type to another, and new or "derived" attributes are defined.

3. **Data Mining** – At this point the data is subjected to one or several data mining methods such as classification, regression, or clustering. In this step, intelligent methods are applied in order to extract data patterns. For extracting the data patterns, it is necessary to may interact with the user or a knowledge base.

4. **Pattern Evaluation** – In this step, data patterns are evaluated to find out the interestingness of the pattern. Sometimes, they are stored as new knowledge in the knowledge base.

5. **Knowledge Presentation** – In this step, visualization and knowledge representation techniques are used to present mined knowledge to users.

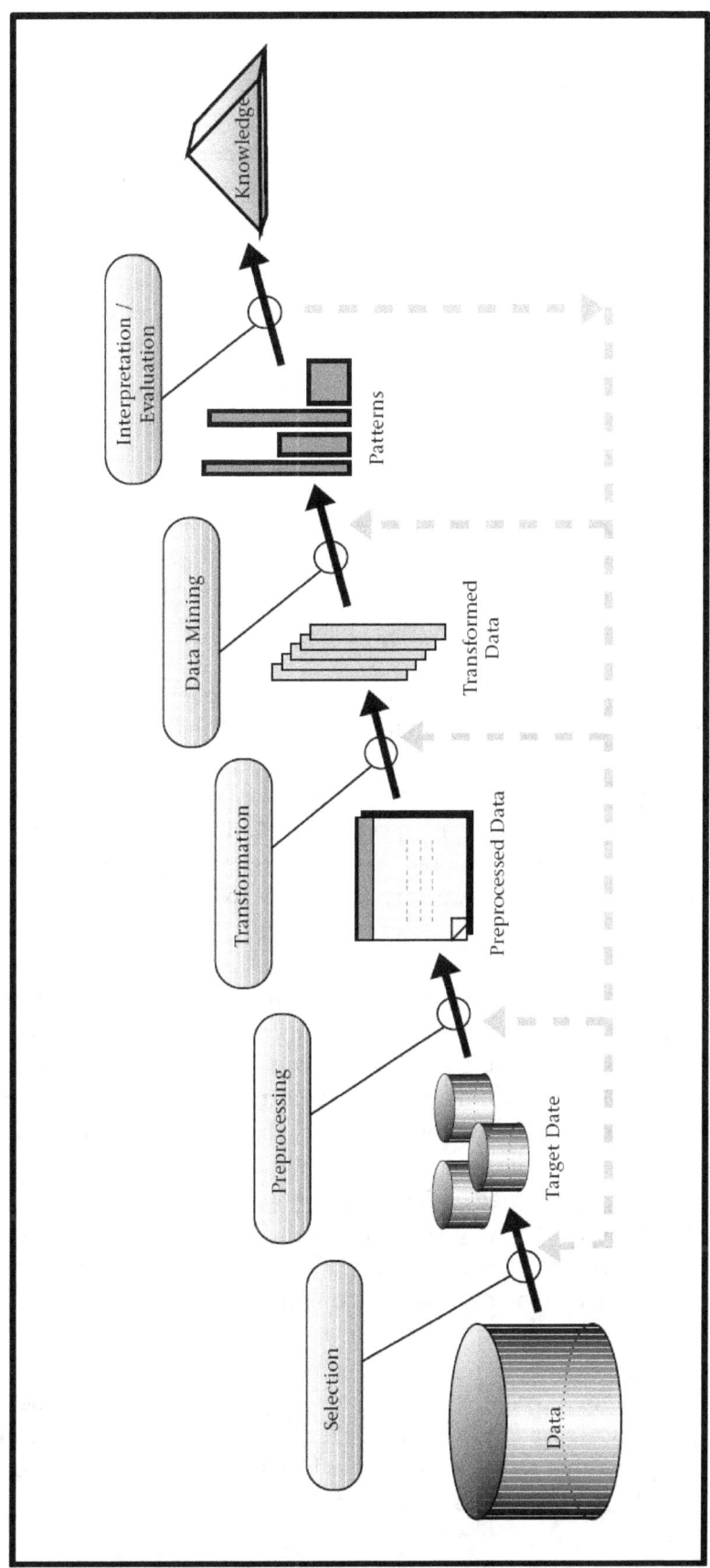

Figure 17: Knowledge Discovery from Data

Q14. What is data cleaning? Describe the different methods of handling missing values during data cleaning.

Real-world data tend to be *incomplete*, *noisy*, and *inconsistent*. Data cleaning (or data cleansing) routines attempt to fill in missing values, smooth out noise while identifying outliers, and correct inconsistencies in the data.

Missing Values:

Imagine that you need to analyze sales and customer data of General Electronics. You note that many tuples have no recorded value for several attributes such as customer income. How can you go about *filling in the missing values* for this attribute? Let's look at the following methods.

1. **Ignore the Tuple (Row)**: This is usually done when the attribute value is missing. This method is not very effective, unless the tuple contains several attributes with missing values. By ignoring the tuple, we do not make use of the remaining attributes values in the tuple. Such data could have been useful to the task at hand.

2. **Fill in the Missing Value Manually**: In general, this approach is time consuming and may not be feasible given a large data set with many missing values.

3. **Use a global constant to fill in the missing value**: Replace all missing attribute values by the same constant such as a label like "Unknown" or 1. If missing values are replaced by, say, "Unknown," then the mining program may mistakenly think that they form an interesting pattern, since they all have a value in common. Hence, although this method is simple, it is not foolproof.

4. **Use a measure of central tendency for the attribute (e.g., the mean or median) to fill in the missing value**: For normal (symmetric) data distributions, the mean can be used, while skewed data distribution should employ the median. For example, suppose that the data distribution regarding the income of General Electronics customers is symmetric and that the mean income is $56,000. Use this value to replace the missing value for income.

5. **Use the attribute mean or median for all samples belonging to the same class as the given tuple:** For example, if classifying customers according to credit risk, we may replace the missing value with the mean income value for customers in the same credit risk category as that of the given tuple. If the data distribution for a given class is skewed, the median value is a better choice.

6. **Use the most probable value to fill in the missing value:** This may be determined with regression, inference-based tools using a Bayesian formalism, or decision tree induction. For example, using the other customer attributes in your data set, you may construct a decision tree to predict the missing values for income.

Q15. What is noise? Explain data smoothing methods used in data cleaning process for noise removal. Divide given data into bins of size 3 by bin partition (equal frequency), by bin means, by bin medians and by bin boundaries. Consider the data: 10, 2, 19, 18, 20, 18, 25, 28, 22.

Noise is a random **error or variance in a measured variable**.

Noisy Data:

Given a numeric attribute such as say, price, how can we **"smooth" out the data** to **0**? We have three techniques for the same:

1. **Binning**
   1.1. **Binning by Mean**
   1.2. **Binning by Median**
   1.3. **Binning by Boundaries**
2. **Regression**
3. **Outlier Analysis**

1. Binning:

Binning methods smooth a sorted data value by consulting its **"neighborhood"**, that is, **the values around it**. Given data is sorted & partitioned into **"buckets"** or **"bins"** of equal size.

1.1. Binning by Mean:
Each value in that bin is replaced by the mean value of that bin.

1.2. Binning by Median:
Each value in that bin is replaced by the median value of that bin.

1.3. Binning by Boundaries:
Here, minimum & maximum values of the bin are identified as the boundaries of that bin. Each value in that bin is replaced by the closest boundary value of that bin.

2. Regression:

Data smoothing can also be done by regression, a technique that **conforms data values to a function**. Linear regression involves **finding the "best" line to fit two attributes** (or variables) so that **one attribute can be used to predict the other**. **Multiple linear regression** is an extension of linear regression, where **more than two attributes are involved** and the data are fit to a **multidimensional surface**.

3. Outlier Analysis:

Outliers may be detected by clustering, for example, where similar v**alues are organized into groups, or "clusters". Values that fall outside of the set of clusters** may be considered outliers.

4. Binning Example:

Data: 10, 2, 19, 18, 20, 18, 25, 28, 22
Sorted Data: 2, 10, 18, 18, 19, 20, 22, 25, 28
Bin Size: 3
Bin A: 2, 10, 18
Bin B: 18, 19, 20
Bin C: 22, 25, 28

Binning by Mean:

Mean A: (02+10+18) / 3 = 10
Mean B: (18+19+20) / 3 = 19
Mean C: (22+25+28) / 3 = 25

Bin A: 10, 10, 10
Bin B: 19, 19, 19
Bin C: 25, 25, 25

Smoothed Data: 10, 10, 10, 19, 19, 19, 25, 25, 25

Binning by Median:

Median A: 10
Median B: 19
Median C: 25

Bin A: 10, 10, 10
Bin B: 19, 19, 19
Bin C: 25, 25, 25

Smoothed Data: 10, 10, 10, 19, 19, 19, 25, 25, 25

Binning by Boundaries:

Boundary A: (2,18)
Boundary B: (18,20)
Boundary C: (22,28)

Bin A: 2, 18, 18
Bin B: 18, 20, 20
Bin C: 22, 28, 28

Smoothed Data: 2, 18, 18, 18, 20, 20, 22, 28, 28

Q16. Explain Mean, Median, Mode, Variance, Standard Deviation with suitable database example.

Mean:

The *sample mean* is the average and is computed as the *sum of all the observed outcomes* from the sample divided by the *total number of events*. We use x as the symbol for the sample mean. In mathematical terms,

$$\overline{X} = \frac{\sum X}{N}$$

Where, Σ = Sum of all…
    X = Member of the data set
    N = Total # items in the data set

One problem with using the mean, is that it often does not depict the typical outcome. If there is one outcome that is very far from the rest of the data, then the mean will be strongly affected because of this outcome. Such an outcome is called and *outlier*.

Median:

The *Median is the middle score*. If we have an even number of events, we take the average of the two middles. The *Median is better than Mean* for describing the typical value.

Suppose you randomly selected 10 house prices in the South Lake area. The prices were: *2.7, 2.9, 3.1, 3.4, 3.7, 4.1, 4.3, 4.7, 4.7, 40.8*. If we computed the mean, we would say that the average house price is 744,000. Although this number is true, it does not reflect the average price for available housing in South Lake area. A closer look at the data shows that the house valued at 40.8 skews the data.

Instead, we use the median. Since there is an even number of outcomes, we take the average of the middle two, that is, 3.9. This better reflects what house shoppers should expect to spend.

Mode:

The *Mode* is another measure of central tendency. The *mode* for a set of data is the *value that occurs most frequently* in the set. In the above example, we consider 4.7 as the mode. A dataset with two or more modes is *multimodal*. At the other end, if each data value occurs only once, then there is *no mode*.

Variance & Standard Deviation:

Variance and standard deviation are measures of *data dispersion*. They indicate how spread out a data distribution is. A *low standard deviation* means that the data observations tend to be very *close to the mean*, while a *high standard deviation* indicates that the data are *spread out over a large range of values*.

The *variance* of N observations, X1, X2, …, XN, is mathematically defined as:

$$s^2 = \frac{\sum (X - \bar{X})^2}{N-1}$$

Where, $\bar{X}$ = the mean value of the observations

X = Member of the data set

N = Total # items in the data set

The *Standard Deviation* of the observations is the *square root of the Variance*. The *Standard Deviation* of n observations, X1, X2, …, Xn, is mathematically defined as:

$$s = \sqrt{\frac{\sum (x - \bar{x})^2}{n-1}}$$

Where, $\bar{X}$ = the mean value of the observations

X = Member of the data set

n = Total # items in the data set

Standard Deviation Example:

The owner of the Indian restaurant is interested in how much people spend at the restaurant. He examines 10 randomly selected receipts and writes down the following data: *44, 50, 38, 96, 42, 47, 40, 39, 46, 50.*

Calculate the spending range of people using the standard deviation.

Mean for the data set = 49.2

X	(X - 49.2) OR (X-X̄)	(X - 49.2)² OR (X-X̄)²
44	-5.2	27.04
50	0.8	0.64
38	11.2	125.44
96	46.8	2190.24
42	-7.2	51.84
47	-2.2	4.84
40	-9.2	84.64
39	-10.2	104.04
46	-3.2	10.24
50	0.8	0.64
	Total:	2600.4

$$ s^2 = \frac{\sum (X - \bar{X})^2}{N - 1} $$

Variance = S^2 = 2600.4 / (10 − 1) = 288.7

Standard Deviation = Square Root (Variance)
                      = Square Root (288.7)
                      = 17

Now, we take the mean and move one standard deviation in either direction. The mean for this example was about 49.2 and the standard deviation was 17. Thus, we get ({49.2 + 17}, {49.2 + 17}) = (32.2, 66.2).

This means that most of the patrons probably spend between $32.20 and $66.20.

Q17. What is data transformation? Explain the different data transformation approaches for transforming data.

In data transformation, the data is consolidated into forms appropriate for mining. Strategies for data transformation include the following:

1. **_Smoothing_**, which works to remove noise from the data. Techniques include binning, regression, and clustering.

2. **_Attribute construction_** (or feature construction), where new attributes are constructed and added from the given set of attributes to help the mining process.

3. **_Aggregation_**, where summary or aggregation operations are applied to the data. For example, the daily sales data may be aggregated so as to compute monthly and annual total amounts. This step is typically used in constructing a data cube for data analysis at multiple abstraction levels.

4. **_Normalization_**, where the attribute data is scaled so as to fall within a smaller range, such as −1.0 to +1.0, or 0.0 to +1.0.

5. **_Discretization_**, where the raw values of a numeric attribute (e.g. age) are replaced by interval labels (e.g., 0–10, 11–20, etc.) or conceptual labels (e.g. youth, adult, senior). The labels, in turn, can be recursively organized into higher-level concepts, resulting in a concept hierarchy for the numeric attribute. Following figure shows a concept hierarchy for the attribute price.

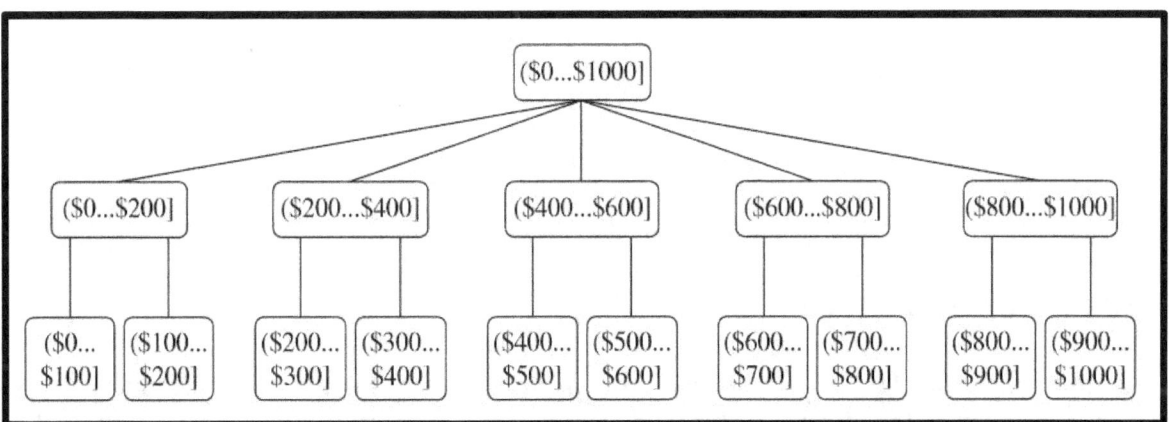

Figure 18: Data Transformation – Discretization – Concept Hierarchy

6. **_Concept hierarchy generation for nominal data_**, where attributes such as street can be generalized to higher-level concepts, like city or country. Many hierarchies for nominal attributes are implicit within the database schema and can be automatically defined at the schema definition level.

Q18. Explain data transformation by normalization. Explain min-max & z-score techniques for normalization.

The ***measurement unit used can affect the data analysis***. For example, changing measurement units from meters to inches for height, or from kilograms to pounds for weight, may lead to very different results. In general, expressing an ***attribute in smaller units*** will lead to a ***larger range for that attribute***, and thus tend to give such attribute a ***greater effect or "weight"***.

To help avoid dependence on the choice of measurement units, the data should be ***normalized or standardized***. This involves transforming the ***data to fall within a smaller or common range*** such as [−1, +1] or [0, +1].

Normalizing the data attempts to give ***all attributes*** an ***equal weight***. Normalization helps prevent attributes with initially large ranges (e.g., income) from outweighing attributes with initially smaller ranges (e.g., binary attributes). There are many methods for data normalization. We'll study ***min-max normalization & z-score normalization***.

Let A be a numeric attribute with n observed values: $v_1, v_2, ..., v_n$.

Min-Max Normalization:

Min-max normalization performs a ***linear transformation*** on the original data. Suppose that min_A and max_A are the minimum and maximum values of an attribute, A. Min-max normalization maps a value, v_i, of A to v_i' in the range [new_min$_A$, new_max$_A$] by computing:

$$v_i' = \frac{v_i - min_A}{max_A - min_A}(new\_max_A - new\_min_A) + new\_min_A.$$

Z-Score Normalization:

In ***z-score normalization*** (or ***zero-mean normalization***), the values for an attribute, A, are normalized ***based on the mean and standard deviation*** of A. A value, v_i, of A is normalized to v_i' by computing:

$$v_i' = \frac{v_i - \bar{A}}{\sigma_A},$$

where $\bar{A}$ and σ_A are the mean and standard deviation, respectively, of attribute A.

Q19. Normalization Example: min-max & z-score.

Minimum salary is 20,000 Rs. and Maximum salary is 1,70,000 Rs.

1. **Map the salary 1,00,000 Rs. in new Range of (60000, 260000) Rs. using min-max normalization method.**

2. **If Mean salary is 54,000 Rs. and standard deviation is 16,000 Rs. then find z score value of 73,600 Rs. salary.**

Answer 1:

Old Range = (20000, 170000)
max = 170000
min = 20000

New Range = (60000, 260000)
new_max = 260000
new_min = 60000

Vi = 100000

Vi' = [{ (vi-min) / (max-min) } * { (new_max - new_min) }] + new_min
= [{ (80000) / (150000) } * (200000)] + 60000
= [106666] + 60000
= 166666

Salary 1,00,000 Rs. In old range is equal to salary 1,66,666 Rs. In the new range.

Answer 2:

Mean = 22,300
Standard Deviation = 16,000

z-score value of 76,300   = (76,300 – Mean) / Standard Deviation
= (22,300) / 16,000
= 1.39

z score value of 73,600 Rs. salary is 1.39.

Q20. Explain Data Reduction Techniques: Data Discretization and Concept Hierarchy Generation, in brief.

Data Reduction obtains a **reduced representation of the data set** that is much smaller in volume, **yet produces the same (or almost the same) analytical results. Discretization** & **Concept Hierarchy Generation** are **data reduction techniques** where **raw data values** for attributes are **replaced by ranges or by conceptual labels**. For example, raw values for age may be replaced by higher-level concepts, such as youth, adult, or senior.

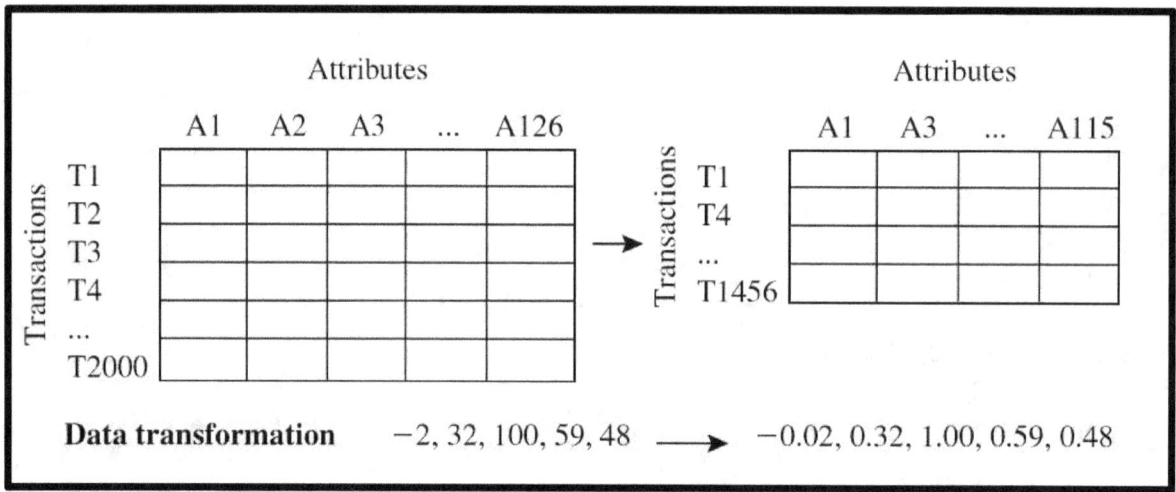

Figure 19: Data Reduction

Data Discretization:

Discretization is a **data reduction technique** where the **raw values of a numeric attribute** (e.g. age) are **replaced by interval labels** (e.g., 0–10, 11–20, etc.). The labels, in turn, can be recursively organized into higher-level concepts, **resulting in a concept hierarchy** for the numeric attribute. Following figure shows a concept hierarchy for the attribute price. More than one concept hierarchy can be defined for the same attribute to accommodate the needs of various users.

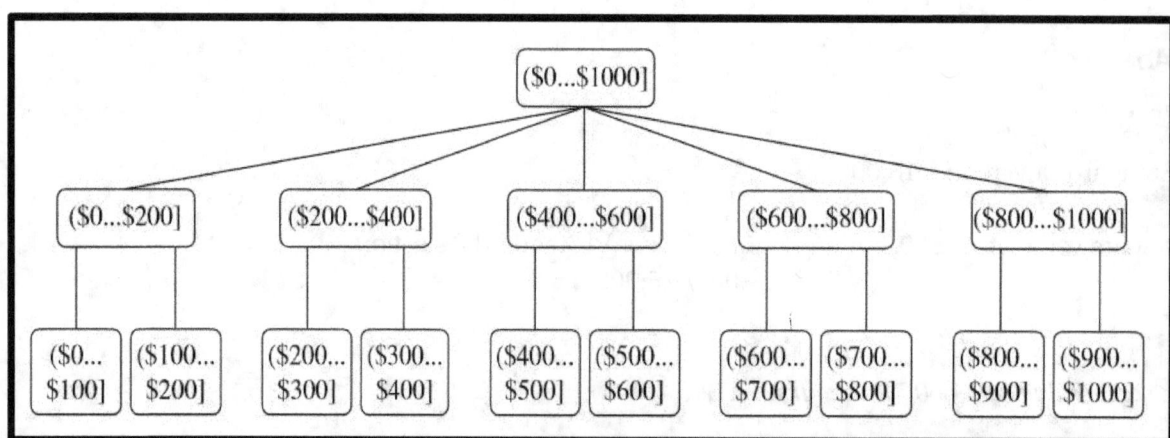

Figure 20: Concept Hierarchy – Data Reduction

Concept Hierarchy Generation:

Concept Hierarchy Generation is a **data reduction technique** where the **raw values of a numeric attribute** (e.g. age) are **replaced by conceptual labels** (e.g. youth, adult, senior). The labels, in turn, can be recursively organized into higher-level concepts, **resulting in a concept hierarchy** for the numeric attribute. Many hierarchies for nominal attributes are implicit within the database schema and can be automatically defined at the schema definition level.

Q21. Explain Data Generalization using attribute oriented induction with a complete example. Show necessary steps.

Data generalization summarizes data by *replacing relatively low-level values (e.g., numeric values for an attribute age) with higher-level concepts (e.g., young, middle-aged, and senior)*, or by *reducing the number of dimensions* to summarize data in concept space involving fewer dimensions. Allowing data sets to be generalized at *multiple levels of abstraction* facilitates users in examining the *general behavior of the data*.

The general idea of *attribute-oriented induction* is to first collect the *task-relevant data* using a *database query* and then perform *generalization* based on the **number of distinct values of each attribute** in the data set.

The *generalization* is performed by either *attribute removal* or *attribute generalization*. *Aggregation* is performed by *merging identical generalized tuples*. This *reduces the size* of the generalized data set.

Example:

A data mining query for characterization. Suppose that a user wants to describe the general characteristics of graduate students in the Big University database, given the attributes name, gender, major, birth place, birth date, residence, phone# (telephone number), and gpa (grade point average). A data mining query for this characterization can be expressed in the data mining query language, DMQL, as follows:

use Big University DB
mine characteristics as "Science Students"
in relevance to name, gender, major, birth place, birth date, residence, phone#, gpa
from student where status in "graduate"

We will see how this example of a typical data mining query can apply attribute-oriented induction to the mining of characteristic descriptions.

A Collection of Task-Relevant Data

name	gender	major	birth_place	birth_date	residence	phone#	gpa
Jim Woodman	M	CS	Vancouver, BC, Canada	12-8-76	3511 Main St., Richmond	687-4598	3.67
Scott Lachance	M	CS	Montreal, Que, Canada	7-28-75	345 1st Ave., Richmond	253-9106	3.70
Laura Lee	F	Physics	Seattle, WA, USA	8-25-70	125 Austin Ave., Burnaby	420-5232	3.83
...	...	...	...	...	...	...	...

Now that the data are ready for attribute-oriented induction, here is how attribute-oriented induction performed: the essential operation of attribute-oriented induction is data generalization, which can be performed in either of two ways on the Task-Relevant Data: ***attribute removal*** and ***attribute generalization***.

<u>**Attribute Removal**</u>: An attribute is removed in the following two circumstances:

- o   There is no concept hierarchy defined for the attribute.

- o   Its higher-level concepts are expressed in terms of other attributes.

<u>***Attribute Generalization***</u>: If there is a ***large set of distinct values for an attribute*** in the Task-Relevant Data, and there exists a concept hierarchy the attribute, then a generalization operator (threshold value for maximum number of distinct values) should be selected and applied to the attribute.

Let's see how both of these techniques are applied on the given example:

1. ***name***: Since there are a large number of distinct values for name and there is no generalization operation defined on it, this attribute is removed.

2. ***gender***: Since there are only two distinct values for gender, this attribute is retained and no generalization is performed on it.

3. ***major***: Suppose that a concept hierarchy has been defined that allows the attribute major to be generalized to the values {arts, sciences, engineering, business}. Suppose also that there are more than 20 distinct values for major in the Task-Relevant Data & the attribute generalization threshold is set to 5. By attribute generalization and attribute generalization control, major is therefore generalized by climbing the given concept hierarchy.

4. ***birth place***: This attribute has a large number of distinct values; therefore, we would like to generalize it. Suppose that a concept hierarchy exists for birth place, defined as "city < province < country." If the number of distinct values for country is less than the attribute generalization threshold, then birth place should be generalized to birth country.

5. ***birth date***: Suppose that a hierarchy exists that can generalize birth date to age and age to age range, and that the number of age ranges (or intervals) is small with respect to the attribute generalization threshold. Generalization of birth date should therefore take place.

6. ***residence***: Suppose that residence is defined by the attributes number, street, residence city, residence province or state, and residence country. The number of distinct values for number and street will likely be very high. The attributes number and street should therefore be removed so that residence is then generalized to residence city, which contains fewer distinct values.

7. ***phone#***: As with the name attribute, phone# contains too many distinct values and should therefore be removed in generalization.

8. ***gpa***: Suppose that a concept hierarchy exists for gpa that groups values for grade point average into numeric intervals like {3.75 – 4.0, 3.5 – 3.75, ...}, which in turn are grouped into descriptive values such as {"excellent", "very good", ...}. The attribute can therefore be generalized.

Generalized Relation Obtained by Attribute-Oriented Induction

gender	major	birth_country	age_range	residence_city	gpa	count
M	Science	Canada	20 – 25	Richmond	very_good	16
F	Science	Foreign	25 – 30	Burnaby	excellent	22
...	...	...	...	...	...	...

Q22. Write Short Note On: Association Rule Mining & Frequent Pattern Mining. Also explain Support and Confidence.

Frequent Item Sets:

Frequent Pattern Mining searches for **relationships among items in large data sets**. To understand **Frequent pattern mining,** we'll begin by presenting an example of market basket analysis, the earliest form of frequent pattern mining for association rules.

Market Basket Analysis:

Market Basket Analysis is a typical example of frequent item set mining. This process analyzes buying habits of the customer by finding associations between the different items that customers place in their "shopping baskets".

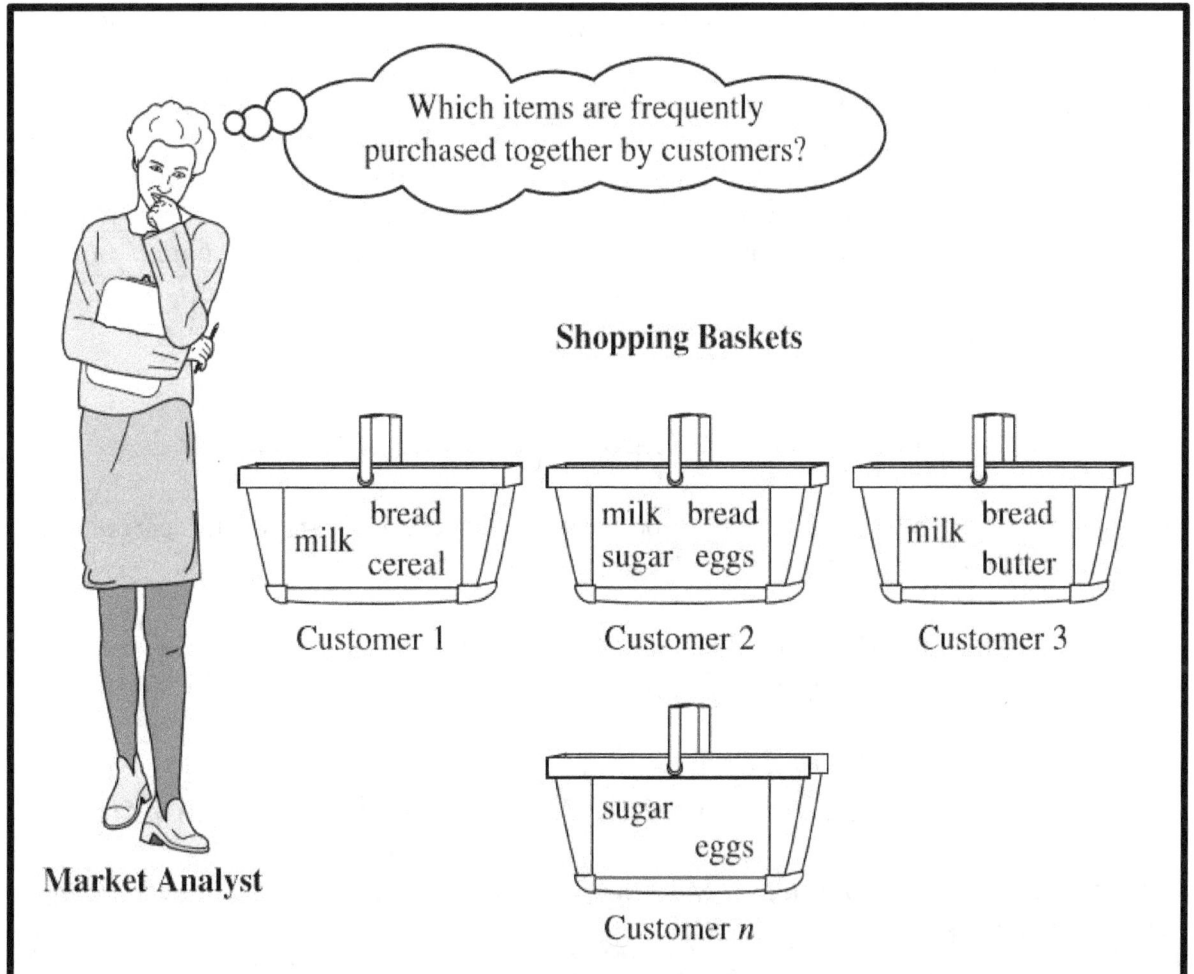

Figure 21: Market Basket Analysis – Frequent Item Set Generation

For instance, if customers are buying milk, how likely are they to also buy bread on the same trip to the supermarket? This information can lead to increased sales by helping retailers do selective marketing and plan their shelf space.

Example: Suppose, as manager of a General Electronics branch, you would like to learn more about the buying habits of your customers. For this, market basket analysis may be performed on the retail data of customer transactions at your store. ***In one strategy***, items that are frequently purchased together can be placed in proximity to further encourage the combined sale of such items. ***In an alternative strategy***, placing frequently purchased items at opposite ends of the store may entice customers who purchase such items to pick up other items along the way.

Association Rules, Support & Confidence:

The **buying patterns** discussed above can be represented in the form of **Association Rules**. For example, the information that customers who purchase computers also tend to buy antivirus software at the same time is represented in the following association rule:

Computer ⇒ antivirus software [support=2%, confidence=60%]

Support and Confidence are two ***measures of rule interestingness***. They, respectively, reflect the usefulness and certainty of the association rules. A support of 2% for a rule means that 2% of all the transactions under analysis show that computer and antivirus software are purchased together. A confidence of 60% means that 60% of the customers who purchased a computer also bought the software. Typically, ***association rules are considered interesting if they satisfy both a minimum support threshold and a minimum confidence threshold.***

An association rule is an implication of the form

A ⇒ B, where A & B ⊂ Item Set, A & B ≠ ∅, and A∩B = ϕ

The rule A ⇒ B holds true in the transaction set with **support s**, where s is the percentage of transactions in the set that contain A ∪ B. This is taken to be the probability, $P(A \cup B)$.

The rule A ⇒ B has **confidence c** in the transaction set, where c is the percentage of transactions in set containing A that also contain B. This is taken to be the conditional probability, $P(B|A)$.

That is,   **support (A ⇒ B) = P (A ∪ B)**
                confidence (A ⇒ B) = P (B|A) = support (A ∪ B) / support (A)

Rules that satisfy both *a minimum support threshold* and *a minimum confidence threshold* are called **Strong Rules**.

In general, association rule mining can be viewed as a two-step process:

1. ***Find all frequent item sets***: By definition, each of these item sets will occur at least as frequently as a predetermined minimum support count.

2. ***Generate strong association rules from the frequent item sets***: By definition, these rules must satisfy minimum support and minimum confidence.

Q23. Explain the following terms: Item Set, Frequent Item Set, & Strong Rule.

A *set of items* is referred to as an **item set**. An item set that contains k items is a *k-item set*. The set *{computer, antivirus software}* is a *2-item set*.

If the *support of an item set* (percentage of transactions in the set that contain all the items of the item set) satisfies a predefined *minimum support threshold*, then the item set is a **frequent item set**.

Association Rules that satisfy both *a minimum support threshold* and *a minimum confidence threshold* are called **Strong Rules**.

Q24. Explain Apriori Algorithm for Frequent Item Set Generation. Explain with example.

The **Apriori Algorithm** is an influential algorithm for **mining frequent item sets** for association rules. Apriori employs an **iterative approach** known as a level-wise search, where k^{th} item set is used to explore $(k+1)^{th}$ item set.

First, the set of frequent 1 item sets is found by scanning the database to accumulate the count for each item, and collecting those items that satisfy minimum support. The resulting set is denoted by L1. Next, L1 is used to find L2, the set of frequent 2-item sets, which is used to find L3, and so on, until no more frequent k-item sets can be found.

Apriori Property: **All nonempty subsets of a frequent item set must also be a frequent item set**.

Consider the following example:

Given below is a database D, consisting of 9 transactions. Suppose that min. support count is 2. Find all the frequent sets using Apriori algorithm.

TID	List of item_IDs
T100	I1, I2, I5
T200	I2, I4
T300	I2, I3
T400	I1, I2, I4
T500	I1, I3
T600	I2, I3
T700	I1, I3
T800	I1, I2, I3, I5
T900	I1, I2, I3

Step 1: Generating 1-itemset Frequent Pattern

	Itemset	Sup.Count
Scan D for count of each candidate	{I1}	6
	{I2}	7
	{I3}	6
	{I4}	2
	{I5}	2

C_1

Compare candidate support count with minimum support count

Itemset	Sup.Count
{I1}	6
{I2}	7
{I3}	6
{I4}	2
{I5}	2

L_1

L1 is the set of frequent 1 – item sets as it consists of the item sets satisfying minimum support.

Step 2: Generating 2-itemset Frequent Pattern

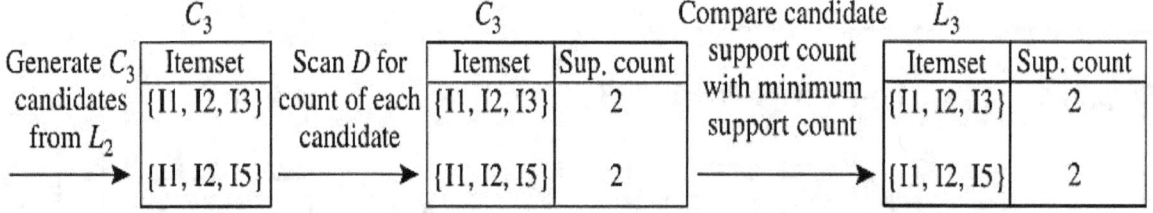

	Itemset		Itemset	Sup. Count		Itemset	Sup Count
Generate C$_2$ candidates from L$_1$	{I1, I2}	Scan D for count of each candidate	{I1, I2}	4	Compare candidate support count with minimum support count	{I1, I2}	4
	{I1, I3}		{I1, I3}	4		{I1, I3}	4
	{I1, I4}		{I1, I4}	1		{I1, I5}	2
	{I1, I5}		{I1, I5}	2		{I2, I3}	4
	{I2, I3}		{I2, I3}	4		{I2, I4}	2
	{I2, I4}		{I2, I4}	2		{I2, I5}	2
	{I2, I5}		{I2, I5}	2		**L$_2$**	
	{I3, I4}		{I3, I4}	0			
	{I3, I5}		{I3, I5}	1			
	{I4, I5}		{I4, I5}	0			
	C$_2$		**C$_2$**				

To discover the set of frequent 2 – item sets, L2, the algorithm uses L1 Join L1 to generate a candidate set of frequent 2 – item sets, C2. Next, the transactions in D are scanned and the support count for each candidate item set in C2 is accumulated. Then we scan C2 & eliminate the item sets with support count less than the minimum threshold. Note: We haven't used Apriori Property yet because each subset of the C2 is also frequent.

Step 3: Generating 3-itemset Frequent Pattern

	C_3		C_3			L_3	
	Itemset		Itemset	Sup. count	Compare candidate support count with minimum support count	Itemset	Sup. count
Generate C_3 candidates from L_2	{I1, I2, I3}	Scan D for count of each candidate	{I1, I2, I3}	2		{I1, I2, I3}	2
	{I1, I2, I5}		{I1, I2, I5}	2		{I1, I2, I5}	2

In order to find C3, we compute L2 Join L2. we first get C3 = L2 join L2 = { **{I1, I2, I3}, {I1, I2, I5}, {I1, I3, I5}, {I2, I3, I4}, {I2, I3, I5}, {I2, I4, I5}** }. Based on the Apriori property that all subsets of a frequent item set must also be frequent, we can determine that the last four candidates cannot possibly be frequent. We therefore remove them from C3, thereby saving the effort of unnecessarily obtaining their counts. This process is called **Pruning**.

We then scan D for the count of remaining two item sets in C3. Then we compare the count values with minimum support count & generate frequent 3 – item set.

Step 4: Generating 4-itemset Frequent Pattern

The algorithm uses L3 Join L3 to generate a candidate set of 4-itemsets, C4. Although the join results in **{ {I1, I2, I3, I5} }**, this item set is pruned since its subset **{ {I2, I3, I5} }** is not frequent.

Thus, C4 =φ, and the algorithm terminates, having found all of the frequent item sets – **L1, L2 & L3**.

Pseudo Code for Apriori Algorithm:

Pass 1

1. Generate the candidate item sets in C_1
2. Save the frequent item sets in L_1

Pass k

1. Generate the candidate item sets in C_k from the frequent item sets in L_{k-1}

   1. Join L_{k-1} with L_{k-1} and insert into C_k

   2. Prune all candidate item sets from C_k where some subset of the candidate item set is not in the frequent item set L_{k-1}

2. Scan the transaction database to determine the support for each candidate item set in C_k

3. Save the frequent item sets in L_k

Q25. Explain Association Rule generation using frequent Item Sets.

Once the frequent item sets from transactions in a database D have been found, it is straightforward to generate strong association rules from them (where strong association rules satisfy both minimum support and minimum confidence). This can be done by calculating the confidence as follows:

$$\text{confidence } (A \Rightarrow B) = P(B|A) = \text{support } (A \cup B) / \text{support } (A)$$

Procedure:

o   For each frequent item set "I", generate all nonempty subsets of I.

o   For every nonempty subset s of I, output the rule "s $\Rightarrow$ (I-s)"

o   If confidence (s $\Rightarrow$ (I-s)) is greater than the minimum confidence threshold, then s $\Rightarrow$ (I-s) is the correct association rule.

Consider the following example:

TID	List of item_IDs
T100	I1, I2, I5
T200	I2, I4
T300	I2, I3
T400	I1, I2, I4
T500	I1, I3
T600	I2, I3
T700	I1, I3
T800	I1, I2, I3, I5
T900	I1, I2, I3

Minimum Confidence is 70%

Going back to the previous example, we had the frequent item set containing: **{ {I1}, {I2}, {I3}, {I4}, {I5}, {I1,I2}, {I1,I3}, {I1,I5}, {I2,I3}, {I2,I4}, {I2,I5}, {I1,I2,I3}, {I1,I2,I5} }**

Let's take a frequent item set, say **{I1, I2, I5}**

The non-empty subsets of X are **{I1, I2}, {I1, I5}, {I2, I5}, {I1}, {I2}**, and **{I5}**

Resulting Association Rules:

$\{I1, I2\} \Rightarrow I5$,   confidence = 2/4 = 50%   <   70%   REJECTED

$\{I1, I5\} \Rightarrow I2$,   confidence = 2/2 = 100%   >   70%   SELECTED

$\{I2, I5\} \Rightarrow I1$,   confidence = 2/2 = 100%   >   70%   SELECTED

$I1 \Rightarrow \{I2, I5\}$,   confidence = 2/6 = 33%   <   70%   REJECTED

$I2 \Rightarrow \{I1, I5\}$,   confidence = 2/7 = 29%   <   70%   REJECTED

$I5 \Rightarrow \{I1, I2\}$,   confidence = 2/2 = 100%   >   70%   SELECTED

Hence, we get ***three strong association rules***.

Q26. Discuss disadvantage of Apriori algorithm. How might the efficiency of Apriori be improved?

Disadvantage:

Apriori algorithm suffers from a number of inefficiencies or trade-offs, which have resulted in creation of other algorithms. **Candidate Set** generation results in **large numbers of subsets** because the algorithm attempts to **load up the candidate set with as many elements as possible** before each scan. This **increases the complexity & reduces the efficiency** of the algorithm.

Improvement in Apriori Algorithm:

Many variations of the Apriori algorithm have been proposed that focus on improving the efficiency of the original algorithm. Several of these variations are summarized as follows:

- o **Hash-Based Technique**: A hash-based technique can be used to reduce the size of the candidate k-item sets, Ck. When scanning each transaction in the database to generate the frequent n-item sets, Ln, we can also generate all the (n+1)-item sets for each transaction, hash (i.e. map) them into the different buckets of a hash table structure, and increase the corresponding bucket counts. A (n+1)-item sets with a corresponding bucket count in the hash table that is below the support threshold cannot be frequent and thus should be removed from the candidate set.

- o **Partitioning**: A partitioning technique requires just two database scans to mine the frequent item sets. It consists of two phases. In phase 1, the algorithm divides the transactions into n nonoverlapping partitions. Then it finds frequent item sets that are local to the partition. A local frequent item set may or may not be frequent with respect to the entire database, D. However, any item set that is potentially frequent with respect to D must occur as a frequent item set in at least one of the partitions.8 Therefore, all local frequent item sets are candidate item sets with respect to D. The collection of frequent item sets from all partitions forms the global candidate item set. In phase 2, a second scan of D is conducted in which the actual support of each candidate is assessed to determine the global frequent item set.

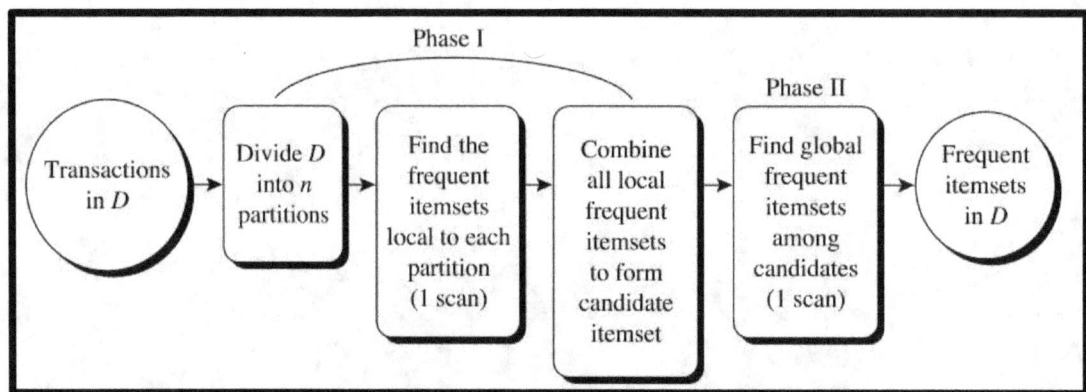

Figure 22: Partitioning the Data - Frequent Set Mining

- o **_Transaction Reduction_**: A transaction that does not contain any frequent k-item sets can not contain any frequent (k+1)-item sets. Therefore, such a transaction can be marked or removed from further consideration

- o **_Sampling_**: The basic idea of the sampling approach is to pick a random sample S of the given data D, and then search for frequent item sets in S instead of D. In this way, we trade off some degree of accuracy against efficiency.

- o **_Dynamic Item Set Counting_**: In this technique, the database is partitioned into blocks marked by start points. Here, a new candidate item set can be added at any start point, unlike in Apriori, which determines new candidate item sets only before a complete database scan. This leads to fewer database scans than with Apriori for finding all the frequent item sets.

Q27. Strong Rules Are Not Necessarily Interesting. Justify.

Whether or not a rule is interesting can be assessed either subjectively or objectively. Ultimately, only the user can judge if a given rule is interesting, and this judgment, being subjective, may differ from one user to another. However, objective interestingness measures, based on the statistics of the data, can be used to weed out uninteresting rules that would otherwise be presented to the user.

Example of a misleading "strong" association rule:

Suppose we are interested in analyzing transactions at General Electronics with respect to the purchase of games and videos. Of the 10,000 transactions analyzed, the data show that 6000 of the customer transactions included games, while 7500 included videos, and 4000 included both games and videos. Considering the minimum support of 30% and a minimum confidence of 60%, the following association rule is discovered:

$$\text{Buys (X, "computer games")} \Rightarrow \text{buys (X, "videos")}$$
$$[\text{support} = 40\%, \text{confidence} = 66\%]$$

The above rule will be reported as a strong association rule because it satisfies the minimum support and minimum confidence thresholds, respectively. However, this rule is misleading because the probability of purchasing videos is 75% (7500 out of 10,000), which is even larger than 66%. Without fully understanding this phenomenon, we could easily make unwise business decisions based on this "Strong Rule".

Hence, we can conclude that **Strong Rules Are Not Necessarily Interesting**.

Q28. What is Classification?

- o A bank loans officer needs analysis of their data to learn which loan applicants are "safe" and which are "risky" for the bank.

- o A marketing manager at General Electronics needs data analysis to help guess whether a customer with a given profile will buy a new computer.

- o A medical researcher wants to analyze breast cancer data to predict which one of three specific treatments a patient should receive.

In each of the above cases, the *data analysis task* is *classification*, where a *classifier* is constructed to *predict class labels*, such as "safe" or "risky" for the loan application data; "yes" or "no" for the marketing data; or "treatment A," "treatment B," or "treatment C" for the medical data.

Data Classification is a *two-step process*, consisting of a *learning step* (where a classification model is constructed) and a *classification step* (where the model is used to predict class labels for given data).

Following is the *example for the loan application data*:

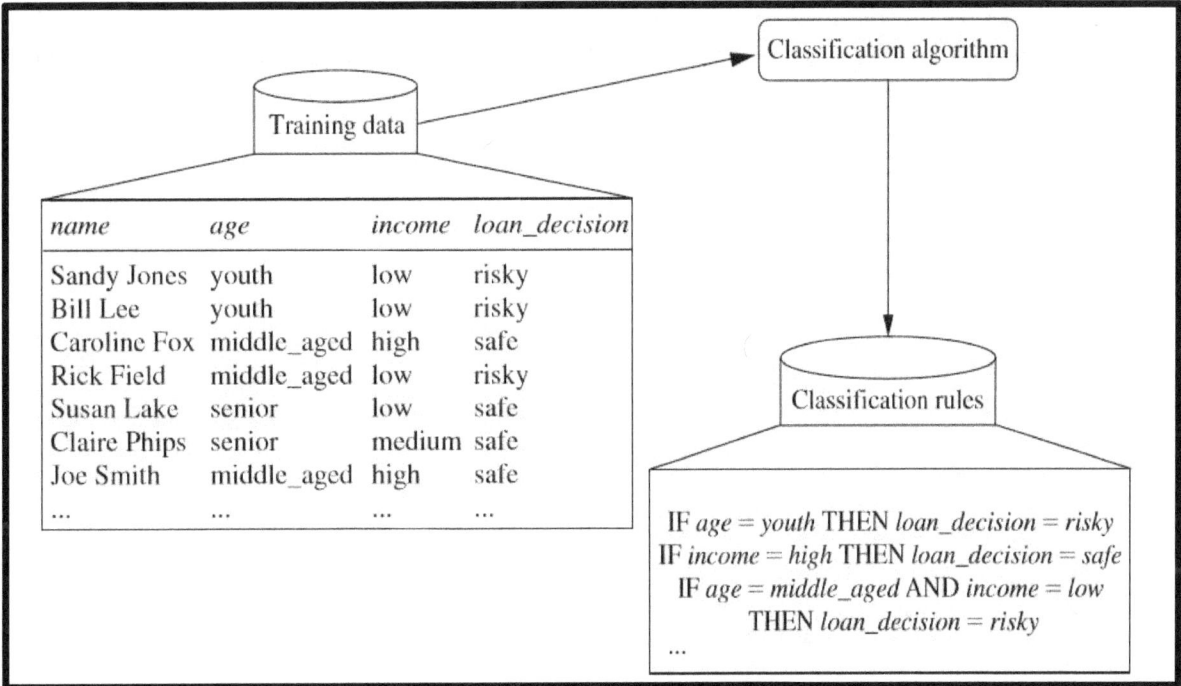

Figure 23: Data Classification – Learning Phase

First step is the *learning step* (or training phase), where a classification algorithm builds the classifier by analyzing a *training set* made up of *database tuples* and their *associated class labels*. The individual tuples making up the training set are referred to as *training tuples* and are randomly sampled from the database under analysis. In the context of classification, *data tuples* can be referred to as *samples, examples, instances, data points, or objects.*

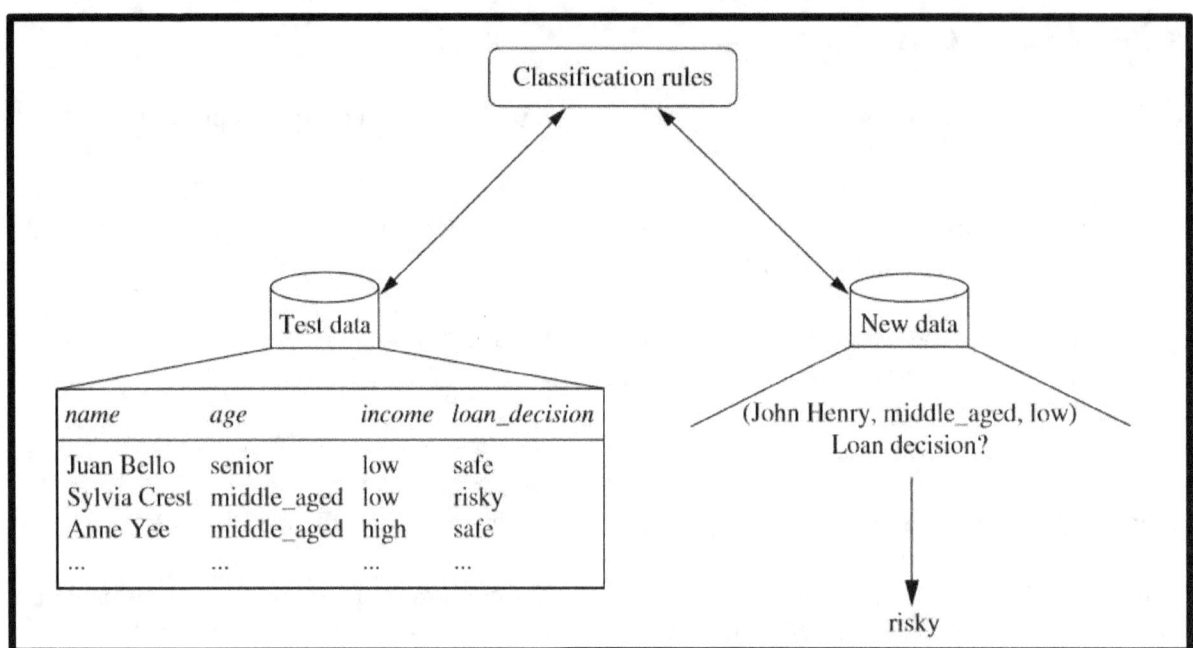

Figure 24: Data Classification – Classification Phase

In the **second step**, the model is used for **classification**. First, the **predictive accuracy** of the classifier is estimated. A **test set** is used, made up of **test tuples** and their **associated class labels**. They are **independent of the training tuples**, meaning that they were not used to construct the **classifier**. The **accuracy of a classifier** on a given test set is the **percentage of test set tuples that are correctly classified by the classifier**.

Q29. What is Decision Tree? Explain the major steps of decision tree induction.

A *decision tree* is a *flowchart-like tree structure*. It breaks down a *training dataset* into smaller and smaller subsets while at the same time an associated decision tree is incrementally developed. Each decision node (non-leaf node) in the tree denotes a test on an attribute, each branch represents an outcome of the test, and each leaf node holds a decision. A typical decision tree is shown below:

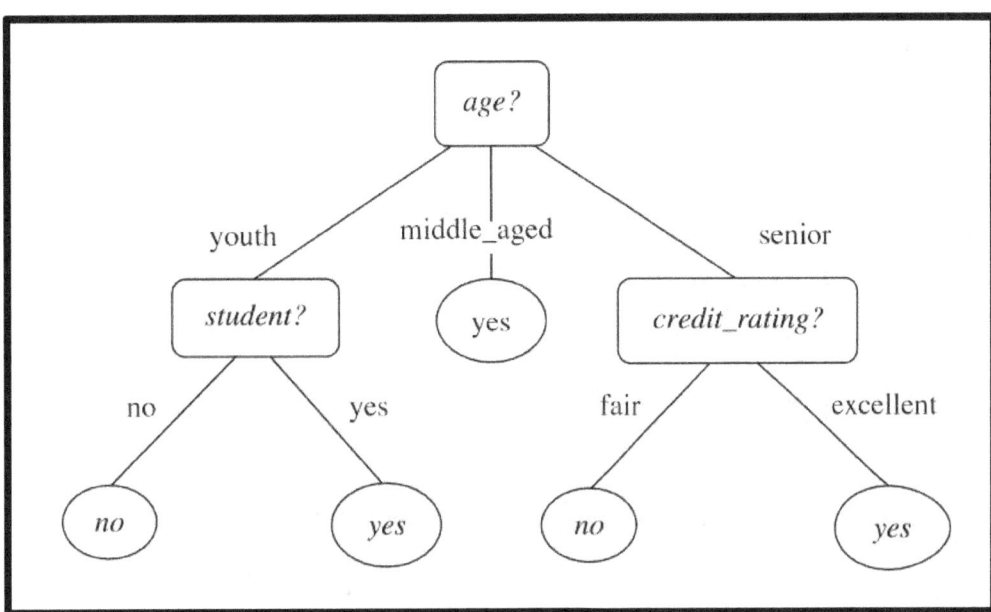

Figure 25: Decision Tree

It represents the concept *'buys computer'*, that is, it predicts whether a customer at General Electronics is likely to purchase a computer or not. Decision nodes are denoted by rectangles, and leaf nodes are denoted by ovals.

The *core algorithm* for building decision trees called *ID3* which employs a *top-down, greedy search* through the space of possible branches with no backtracking. *ID3* uses *Entropy* & *Information Gain* to construct a decision tree.

Please
Turn
Over

Predictors				Target
Outlook	**Temp**	**Humidity**	**Windy**	**Hours Played**
Rainy	Hot	High	False	26
Rainy	Hot	High	True	30
Overcast	Hot	High	False	48
Sunny	Mild	High	False	46
Sunny	Cool	Normal	False	62
Sunny	Cool	Normal	True	23
Overcast	Cool	Normal	True	43
Rainy	Mild	High	False	36
Rainy	Cool	Normal	False	38
Sunny	Mild	Normal	False	48
Rainy	Mild	Normal	True	48
Overcast	Mild	High	True	62
Overcast	Hot	Normal	False	44
Sunny	Mild	High	True	30

Figure 26: Training Data Set for Decision Tree Induction

Steps for Decision Tree Construction (using ID3):

1. *To build a decision tree, we need to calculate two types of entropy using frequency tables as follows:*

   a. *Entropy using the frequency table of one attribute:*

   $$E(S) = \sum_{i=1}^{c} - p_i \log_2 p_i$$

   Where,   S: attribute in a training dataset

   c: number of classes (distinct values) in training dataset for an attribute S

   pi: number of values of class i of attribute S

PlayGolf		
Yes	No	Total
9	5	14

Entropy (PlayGolf)

$$= -\frac{9}{14} \log_2 \left(\frac{9}{14}\right) - \frac{5}{14} \log_2 \left(\frac{5}{14}\right)$$

$$= 0.940$$

b. Entropy using the frequency table of two attributes:

$$E(T,X) = \sum_{c \in X} P(c)E(c)$$

Where,   T: attribute 1 in a training dataset

X: attribute 2 in a training dataset

c: classes (distinct values) in training dataset for an attribute X

P(c): Probability of cth class of attribute X. It is ratio of number of occurrences of c to the total occurrences in X

E(c): Entropy of cth class

		Play Golf		
		Yes	No	
	Sunny	3	2	5
Outlook	Overcast	4	0	4
	Rainy	2	3	5
				14

$E\ (PlayGolf, Outlook)$

$= P(Sunny) * E\left(\frac{3}{5}, \frac{2}{5}\right) + P(overcast) * E\left(\frac{4}{4}, 0\right)$

$\qquad\qquad\qquad + P(Rainy) * E\left(\frac{2}{5}, \frac{3}{5}\right)$

$= \left(\frac{5}{14}\right) * 0.971 + \left(\frac{4}{14}\right) * 0 + \left(\frac{5}{14}\right) * 0.971$

$= 0.693$

2. **After calculating the entropy of the target (Play Golf), the dataset is then split on the different attributes – (Play Golf, Outlook), (Play Golf, Temp.), (Play Golf, Humidity), (Play Golf, Windy). Then, Noise Gain is calculated for each of these attributes.**

$$Gain(T,X) = Entropy(T) - Entropy(T,X)$$

		Play Golf	
		Yes	No
Outlook	Sunny	3	2
	Overcast	4	0
	Rainy	2	3
Gain = 0.247			

		Play Golf	
		Yes	No
Temp.	Hot	2	2
	Mild	4	2
	Cool	3	1
Gain = 0.029			

		Play Golf	
		Yes	No
Humidity	High	3	4
	Normal	6	1
Gain = 0.152			

		Play Golf	
		Yes	No
Windy	False	6	2
	True	3	3
Gain = 0.048			

3. **Attribute with the largest information gain is selected as the decision node. Then, the dataset is divided by its branches and same process is repeated on every branch.**

4. **A branch with entropy of 0 is a leaf node. A branch with entropy more than 0 needs further splitting. After further splitting of Outlook, following will be the decision tree:**

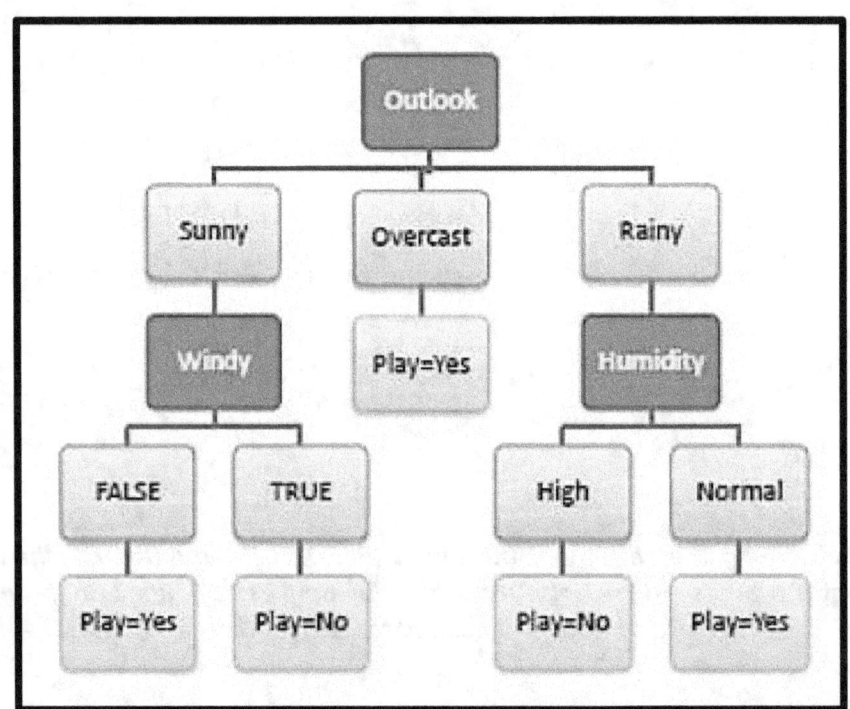

Q30. Explain the following attribute selection measures: Information Gain, Gain Ratio & Gini Index.

An ***attribute selection measure*** is a ***method for selecting the splitting criteria*** that "best" separates a given data partition, D.

The ***attribute selection measure*** provides a ***ranking for each attribute*** describing the given training dataset. The ***attribute having the best score*** for the measure is chosen as the ***splitting attribute*** for the given tuples. ***Attribute selection measures*** are also known as ***splitting rules*** because they determine how the tuples at a given node are to be split.

Attribute selection measures are generally used for ***construction of decision trees***. ***ID3*** uses ***information gain*** as its ***attribute selection measure***.

Please
Turn
Over

Information Gain:

The term information gain & entropy are related to each other. The entropy characterizes the impurity of an arbitrary collection of data. Information Gain is the expected reduction in entropy caused by partitioning the examples according to a given attribute.

To find the information gain, we first need to find out the entropy of an attribute. It can be done as follows.

1. *Entropy using the frequency table of one attribute:*

$$E(S) = \sum_{i=1}^{c} - p_i \log_2 p_i$$

Where,   S: attribute in a training dataset
                   c: number of classes (distinct values) in training dataset for an attribute S
                   pi: number of values of class i of attribute S

2. *Entropy using the frequency table of two attributes:*

$$E(T,X) = \sum_{c \in X} P(c)E(c)$$

Where,   T: attribute 1 in a training dataset
                   X: attribute 2 in a training dataset
                   c: classes (distinct values) in training dataset for an attribute X
                   E(c): Entropy of cth class
                   P(c): Probability of cth class of attribute X. It is ratio of number of occurrences of c to the total occurrences in X

3. *Information Gain:*

$$Gain(T,X) = Entropy(T) - Entropy(T,X)$$

Example:

	Predictors			Target
Outlook	**Temp.**	**Humidity**	**Windy**	**Hours Played**
Rainy	Hot	High	False	26
Rainy	Hot	High	True	30
Overcast	Hot	High	False	48
Sunny	Mild	High	False	46
Sunny	Cool	Normal	False	62
Sunny	Cool	Normal	True	23
Overcast	Cool	Normal	True	43
Rainy	Mild	High	False	36
Rainy	Cool	Normal	False	38
Sunny	Mild	Normal	False	48
Rainy	Mild	Normal	True	48
Overcast	Mild	High	True	62
Overcast	Hot	Normal	False	44
Sunny	Mild	High	True	30

Training Data Set

PlayGolf		
Yes	No	Total
9	5	14

Entropy (PlayGolf)

$$= -\frac{9}{14} \log_2 \left(\frac{9}{14}\right) - \frac{5}{14} \log_2 \left(\frac{5}{14}\right)$$

$$= 0.940$$

		Play Golf		
		Yes	No	
Outlook	Sunny	3	2	5
	Overcast	4	0	4
	Rainy	2	3	5
				14

$$E\ (PlayGolf,\ Outlook)$$
$$= P(Sunny) * E\left(\frac{3}{5}, \frac{2}{5}\right) + P\ (overcast) * E\left(\frac{4}{4}, 0\right)$$
$$+ P\ (Rainy) * E\left(\frac{2}{5}, \frac{3}{5}\right)$$
$$= \left(\frac{5}{14}\right) * 0.971 + \left(\frac{4}{14}\right) * 0 + \left(\frac{5}{14}\right) * 0.971$$
$$= 0.693$$

Gain (Play Golf, Outlook)   **= Entropy (Play Golf) – Entropy (Play Golf, Outlook)**
                                  = 0.940 - 0.693
                                  = 0.247

Gain Ratio:

C4.5, a **successor of ID3**, uses an extension to information gain known as **gain ratio**, which attempts to **overcome the biasness** towards multi-valued attributes that occurs **in information gain**. It applies normalization to information gain using a "split information" value defined as:

$$SplitInfo_A(D) = -\sum_{j=1}^{v} \frac{|D_j|}{|D|} \times \log_2 \left(\frac{|D_j|}{|D|} \right)$$

Where,   A = Attribute of the dataset
D = Dataset
v = Number of classes in attribute A
Dj = Number of values belonging to j[th] class of attribute A
D = Total values in attribute A

$$GainRatio(A) = \frac{Gain(A)}{SplitInfo_A(D)}$$

Gini Index:

The Gini index is used In CART classification. Using the notation previously described, the Gini index measures the impurity of a data partition (D) as:

$$Gini(D) = 1 - \sum_{i=1}^{m} p_i^2$$

Example:

PlayGolf		
Yes	No	Total
9	5	14

Gini (Play Golf)   = 1 – (9/14)² – (5/14)²
                               = 0.459

Q31. Explain CART Classification Method.

Decision Trees are commonly used in data mining with the objective of creating a model that **predicts the value of a target** based on the values of several input.

CART stands for **Classification and Regression Trees**. It is a methodology used to refer to the following types of decision trees:

1. **Classification Trees**: where the target variable is categorical and the tree is used to identify the "class" within which a target variable would likely fall into.

2. **Regression Trees**: where the target variable is continuous and tree is used to predict it's value.

The **CART algorithm** is structured as a **sequence of questions**, the answers to which determine what the next question, if any should be. The **result** of these questions is a **tree like structure** where the ends are terminal nodes at which point there are no more questions.

The representation for the **CART model** is a **binary tree**. Each **root node** represents a **single input variable (x)** and a **split point** on that variable. The leaf nodes of the tree contain an **output variable (y)** which is used to make a prediction.

The **main elements of CART** (and any decision tree algorithm) are:

1. *Rules for splitting data at a node based on the value of one variable*

2. *Stopping rules for deciding when a branch is terminal and can be split no more*

3. *Finally, a prediction for the target variable in each terminal node.*

Given a dataset with two inputs - **height in centimeters** and **weight in kilograms**, prediction for the output of **sex as male or female** is performed. Below is an example of a **binary decision tree** for the same:

PLEASE TURN OVER

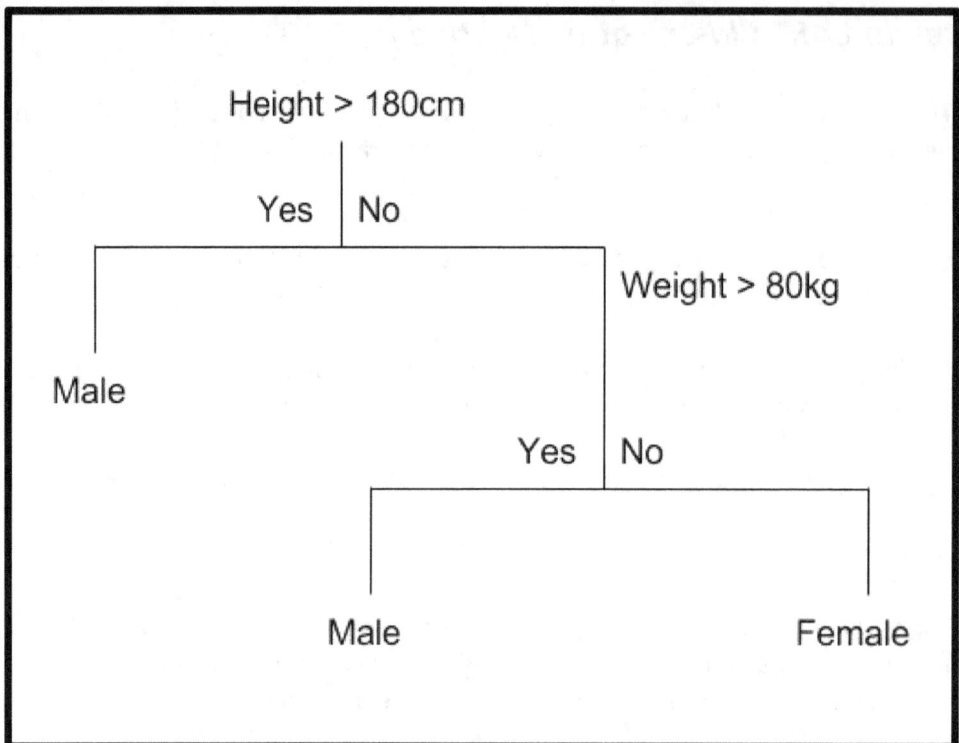

Figure 27: CART - Decision Tree

The *tree* can be stored to file as a graph or a *set of rules*. For example, below is the above decision tree as a set of rules:

1. **If Height > 180 cm Then Male**
2. **If Height <= 180 cm AND Weight > 80 kg Then Male**
3. **If Height <= 180 cm AND Weight <= 80 kg Then Female**

With the *binary tree representation* of the CART model described above, making *predictions is relatively straightforward*. Given a new input, the tree is traversed by evaluating the specific input started at the root node of the tree. The leaf node of the tree gives the required output.

Q32. Write a note on Naive Bayesian classification.

The **Naive Bayesian Classifier** makes the assumption of **class conditional independence**, that is, given the class label of a tuple, the **values of the attributes** are assumed to be **conditionally independent of one another**. This simplifies computation. However, in practice, the dependencies can exist between variables. This is why the Bayesian classifier is considered **"naïve".**

Bayesian belief networks specify joint **conditional probability distributions**. They allow **class conditional independencies** to be defined between subsets of variables. They provide a **graphical model** of causal **relationships**, on which learning can be performed. A belief network is defined by two components—a **directed acyclic graph** and a set of **conditional probability tables.**

Bayesian belief networks can also be used for **classification**. In Bayesian terms, **X** is considered "**evidence**" & is described by measurements made on a **set of n attributes**.

Let **H** be some **hypothesis**, such as that the **data tuple X belongs to a specified class C**. For classification problems, we want to determine **P(H|X)**, the probability that the hypothesis H holds given the "evidence". In other words, we are looking for the probability that tuple X belongs to class C, given that we know the attribute description of X.

Posterior probability:

P(H|X) is the **posterior probability** of **H conditioned on X**.

For example, suppose our set of data tuples is confined to customers described by the attributes age and income, respectively, and that **X is a 35-year-old customer with an income of $40,000**.

Suppose that **H is the hypothesis** that our **customer will buy a computer**. Then **P(H|X)** reflects the **probability** that customer X will buy a computer, given that we know the customer's age and income.

Similarly, **P(X|H)** is the **posterior probability** of **X conditioned on H**. That is, it is the probability that a customer, X, is 35 years old and earns $40,000, given that we know the **customer will buy a computer**.

Prior probability:

P(H) is the **prior probability** of **H. For example**, this is the probability that any given customer will buy a computer, regardless of age, income, or any other information, for that matter.

The posterior probability, P(H|X), is based on more information (e.g., customer information) than the prior probability, P(H).

P(X) is the prior probability of X. Using our example, it is the probability that a person from our set of customers is 35 years old and earns $40,000.

P(H), P(X|H), and P(X) may be estimated from the given data. **Bayes' theorem** is useful in calculating the posterior probability, P(H|X), from P(H), P(X|H), and P(X). Bayes' theorem is:

$$P(H|X) = \frac{P(X|H)P(H)}{P(X)}.$$

Effectiveness of Naïve Bayesian Classification:

In theory, **Bayesian classifiers** have the **minimum error rate** in comparison to all other classifiers. However, in practice this is not always the case, owing to **inaccuracies in the assumptions** made for its use, such as class conditional independence, and the **lack of available probability data**. Although, Bayesian classifiers provide a **theoretical justification** for other classifiers that do not explicitly use Bayes' theorem.

Q33. Explain Rule Based Classification.

Rule-based classifier makes use of a **set of 'IF-THEN' rules** for classification. We can express a rule in the following from:

IF condition THEN conclusion

Let us consider a rule R1,

**R1: IF age = youth AND student = yes
THEN buy_computer = yes**

The IF part of the rule is called rule **antecedent** or **precondition**.

The THEN part of the rule is called rule **consequent**.

The **antecedent** part the condition consist of one or more **attribute tests** and these tests are **logically ANDed**.

The **consequent** part consists of **class prediction**.

We can also write rule R1 as follows:

R1: (age = youth) ^ (student = yes) --> (buys_computer = yes)

If the condition in a rule antecedent holds true for a given tuple, we say that the rule antecedent is satisfied and that the rule covers the tuple.

A rule R can be assessed by its **coverage** and **accuracy**. Given a tuple, X, from a class labeled dataset, D, let n_{covers} be the number of tuples covered by R; $n_{correct}$ be the number of tuples correctly classified by R; and |D| be the number of tuples in D. We can define the coverage and accuracy of R as:

$$coverage(R) = \frac{n_{covers}}{|D|}$$

$$accuracy(R) = \frac{n_{correct}}{n_{covers}}$$

That is, a **rule's coverage** is the percentage of tuples that are covered by the rule (i.e. their attribute values hold true for the rule's antecedent).

For a **rule's accuracy**, we look at the tuples that it covers and see what percentage of them the rule can correctly classify.

Q34. What is Regression? Explain Linear Regression and Non-linear Regression techniques of prediction.

Regression is a data mining *function that predicts a number*. Age, weight, distance, temperature, income, or sales could all be predicted using regression techniques. For example, a regression model could be used to predict children's height, given their age, weight, and other factors.

A *regression task* begins with a *data set* in which the *target values are known*. For example, a regression model that predicts children's height could be developed based on *observed data for many children over a period of time*. The data might track age, height, weight, developmental milestones, family history, and so on. *Height would be the target, the other attributes would be the predictors*, and the *data for each child would constitute a case*.

Regression is the process of estimating the value of a continuous target (y) as a function (F) of one or more predictors (x1, x2, ..., xn), a set of parameters (θ1, θ2, ..., θn), and a measure of error (e).

$$y = F(x, \theta) + e$$

The process of *training a regression model* involves *finding the best parameter values* for the function that *minimize a measure of the error*.

Linear Regression:

The simplest form of regression to visualize is linear regression with a single predictor. A linear regression technique can be used if the relationship between x and y can be approximated with a straight line. Linear regression with a single predictor can be expressed with the following equation:

$$y = \theta2x + \theta1 + e$$

The regression parameters in simple linear regression are:

1. *The slope of the line (θ_2)* — The angle between a data point and the regression line.

2. *The y intercept (θ_1)* — The point where x crosses the y axis (x = 0)

Non-Linear Regression:

Often the relationship between x and y cannot be approximated with a straight line. In this case, a nonlinear regression technique may be used. Alternatively, the data could be preprocessed to make the relationship linear.

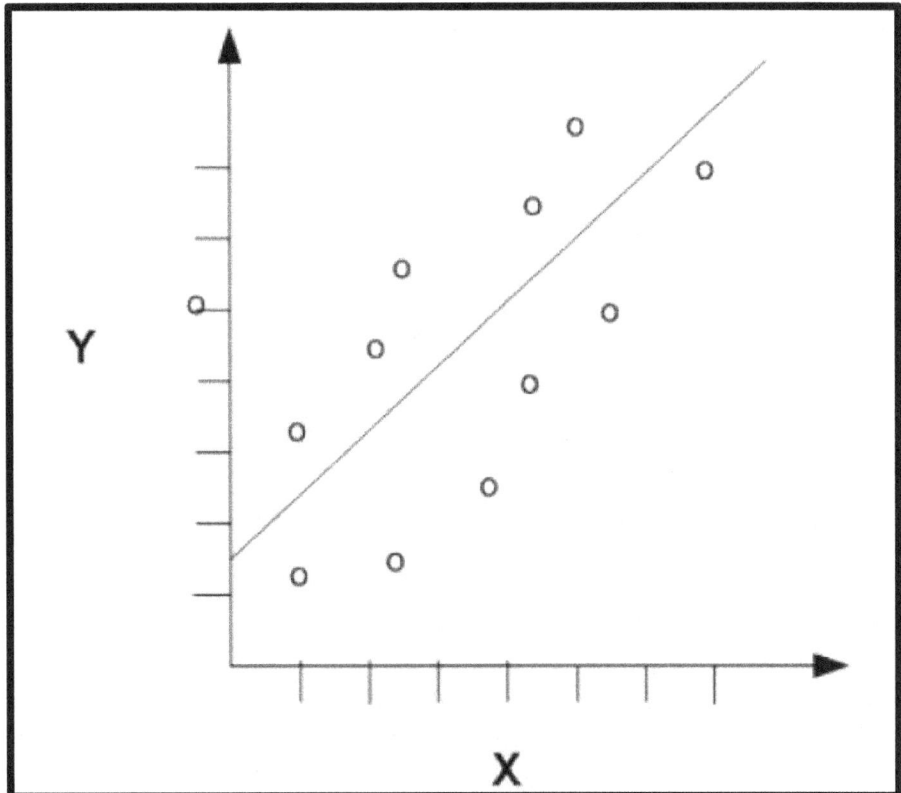

Figure 28: Linear Regression – Prediction

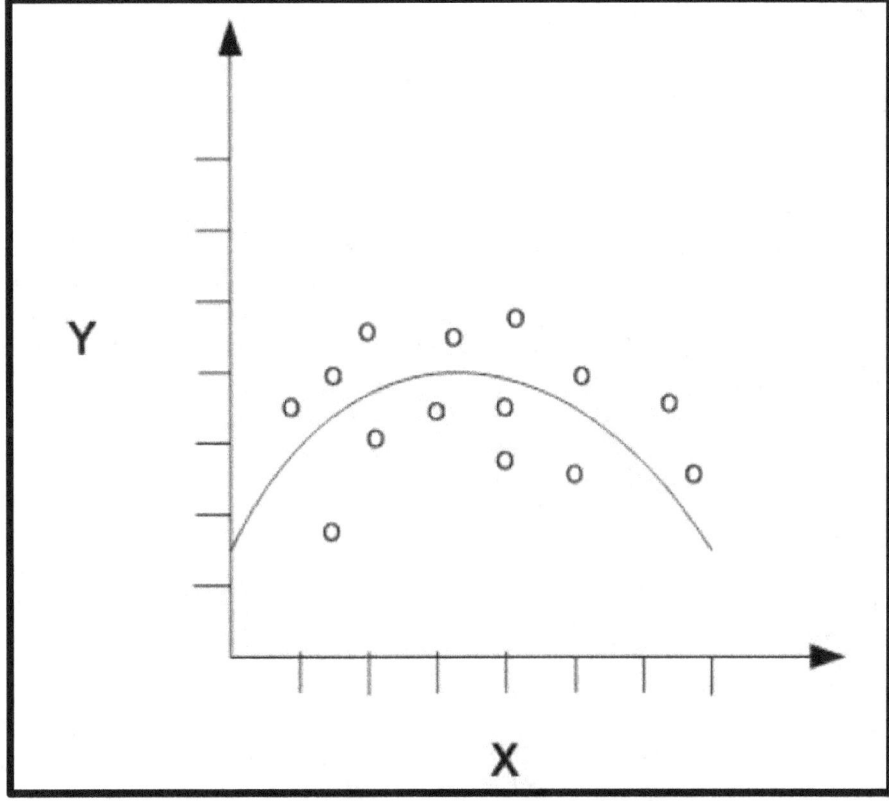

Figure 29: Non-Linear Regression – Prediction

Q35. Define the differences between:

i. Classification and Clustering:

Classification	Clustering
There is a prior knowledge of classes.	There is no prior knowledge of classes.
Classification is a supervised learning technique.	Classification is a unsupervised learning technique.
Classification uses the algorithms to categorize the new data in to classes, according to the observations of the training set.	Clustering uses statistical concepts to split the datasets into subsets with similar features.
Algorithms Used: Decision Tree, Bayesian Classifier	Algorithms Used: K-Means, Expectation Maximization
Requires training dataset containing labeled data.	Requires unlabeled data samples.
The aim of classification is to find which class a new object belongs to from the set of predefined classes.	The aim of clustering is, grouping a set of objects in order to find whether there is any relationship between them.

ii. Classification and Prediction:

Classification	Prediction
Classification models predicts categorical class labels.	Prediction models predicts the numeric values of the class labels.
It is applied on the existing data; no new data is generated.	It is used to predict the new data by analyzing the patterns in the existing data.
For instance, we can build a classification model to categorize bank loan applications as either safe or risky.	For instance, we can use the prediction model to predict the expenditures in dollars of potential customers.
Classification is performed using Decision Trees	Prediction is performed using Regression

Q36. What is Business Intelligence? Explain Business Intelligence in today's perspective.

While there are varying definitions for **Business Intelligence**, Forrester defines it broadly as a **"set of methodologies, processes, architectures, and technologies that transform raw data into meaningful and useful information that allows business users to make informed business decisions"**.

In other words, the high-level goal of **Business Intelligence** is to help a business user turn business-related **data into actionable knowledge**.

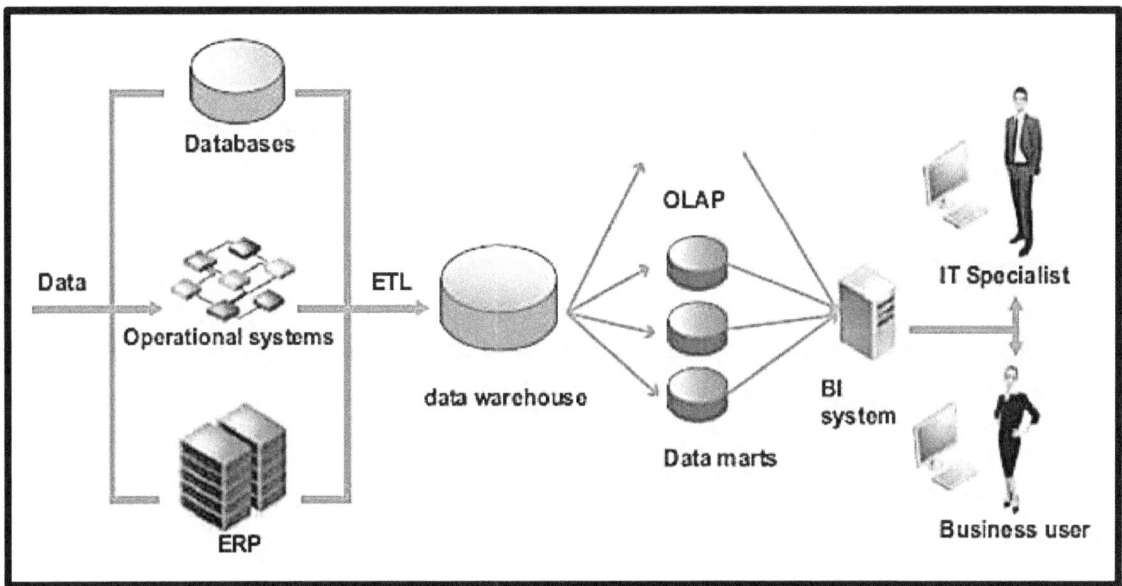

Figure 30: Architecture of Business Intelligence

BI **traditionally** focused on reports, dashboards, and answering predefined questions. But in **today's perspective**, BI also includes a focus on **deeper, exploratory, and interactive analyses of the data** using Business Analytics such as **data mining, predictive analytics, statistical analysis**, and **natural language processing** solutions.

BI systems evolved by adding **layers of data staging** to increase the accessibility of the business data to business users.

- o **Data** from the operational systems and ERP were extracted, **transformed into a more consumable form**, & **stored into data warehouses**.

- o Data from a warehouse were then **loaded into data marts**, as well as **OLAP cubes** which facilitated the **analysis of data over several dimensions**.

- o **Data marts** present a subset of the warehouse data, **tailored to a specific line of business**.

Using Business Intelligence system, the business user, with the help of an IT specialist who had set up the system for her, could now more **easily access and analyze the data**.

Q37. Explain Big Data & Characteristics of Big Data (V3s) in brief.

'Big Data' is similar to 'small data', but bigger in size. But having data bigger, it *requires different approaches*: Techniques, tools and architecture.

Big Data generates value from the *storage and processing of very large quantities of digital information* that cannot be analyzed with traditional computing techniques.

Like many new information technologies, big data can bring about *dramatic cost reductions*, *substantial improvements in the time required to perform a computing task*, or new product and service offerings. It can be the *next big thing* in the *IT industry*.

The first organizations to embrace Big Data were *online firms* and *startup firms*.

Firms like *Google, eBay, LinkedIn, & Facebook* were built around *big data* since the very beginning.

Examples of Big Data:

o   *Walmart* handles more than 1 million customer transactions every hour.

o   *Facebook* handles 40 billion photos from its user base.

o   Decoding the *human genome* originally took 10 years to process; now it can be achieved in one week.

o   *Twitter* generates 7TB of data daily.

o   *IBM* claims 90% of today's stored data was generated in just the last two years.

How Is Big Data Different?

o   Automatically generated by a machine (e.g. Sensor embedded in an engine).

o   Typically, an entirely new source of data (e.g. Use of the internet).

o   Not designed to be friendly (e.g. Text streams).

o   May not have much values need to focus on the important part.

Three Characteristics of Big Data (V3s):

Three major characteristics of Big Data are: ***Volume, Velocity, & Variety***

Volume:

- o A typical PC might have had 10 gigabytes of storage in 2000.

- o Today, Facebook ingests 500 terabytes of new data every day.

- o Boeing 737 will generate 240 terabytes of flight data during a single flight across the US.

- o The smart phones, the data they create and consume; sensors embedded into everyday objects will soon result in billions of new, constantly-updated data feeds containing environmental information, geographical location, and other information, including videos.

Velocity:

- o Clickstreams and ad impressions capture user behavior at millions of events per second

- o High-frequency stock trading algorithms reflect market changes within microseconds

- o Machine to machine processes exchange data between billions of devices

- o Infrastructure and sensors generate massive log data in real-time

- o On-line gaming systems support millions of concurrent users, each producing multiple inputs per second.

Variety:

- o Big Data isn't just numbers, dates, and strings. Big Data is also geospatial data, 3D data, audio and video, and unstructured text, including log files and social media.

- o Traditional database systems were designed to address smaller volumes of structured data, fewer updates or a predictable, consistent data structure.

- o Big Data analysis includes different types of data.

Q38. Define the terms: Clustering, Spatial mining, Web mining, Text mining.

Clustering:

Cluster is a group of objects that belongs to the same class. In other words, similar objects are grouped in one cluster and dissimilar objects are grouped in another cluster. **Clustering** is a process of partitioning a set of data (or objects) into a set of meaningful sub-classes, called clusters.

Spatial Mining:

Spatial data mining is the application of data mining to **spatial models**. In spatial data mining, analysts use **geographical or spatial information** to produce business intelligence or other results. This requires specific techniques and resources to get the geographical data into relevant and useful formats.

Web Mining:

Web mining is the use of data mining techniques to **automatically** discover and extract information from **Web documents and services**. There are three general classes of information that can be discovered by web mining: **Web Activity**, **From Server Logs** and **Web Browser Activity Tracking**.

Text Mining:

Text mining, also referred to as **text data mining**, refers to the process of **deriving high-quality information from text**. High-quality information is typically derived through the **devising of patterns and trends** through means such as **statistical pattern learning**.